$6.10

D0168639

LEADERSHIP, MANAGEMENT

and the Five Essentials for Success

RICK JOYNER

MorningStar
PUBLICATIONS
16000 Lancaster Highway • Charlotte, NC 28277-2061

ISBN 1-878327-33-X

Distributed by:

MorningStar Publications
16000 Lancaster Hwy.
Charlotte, North Carolina 28277-2061
(704) 542-0278

Table of Contents

Chapter 1   **The Fundamentals of Leadership**   **9**

Leadership vs Management   10
The Gauntlet   12
The Essential Partnership   13
Management Based Leadership   14
Peace of Mind—The Foundation for Victory   16
Arrogance—The Foundation for Defeat   16
Crisis—The Cocoon of the Great   17
Defeat—The Foundation for Future Victory   20

Chapter 2   **The Titanic Syndrome**   **23**

Chapter 3   **You Are Here**   **31**

The Four Great Epochs of History   31
A Foundation for Understanding the Future   33
Understanding Economic War   34
A New Breed of Leader   35
The Price of Change   37
God Save Democracy   39
A New Democracy   40
The Alternatives   42
The Nature of Freedom   44
We Must Not Forget People   46

Chapter 4   **The Vision and the Plan—
The Two Pillars of Leadership**   **49**

Having a Vision, Being Goal Oriented   49
Cultivating Vision   51
The Ability to Formulate a Plan   54

Chapter 5   **Character, Will and Wisdom**   **57**

The Will to Implement the Plan   57
Keeping Priorities   58
Steadfastness   61

	Endurance	63
	Integrity	64
	Courage	66
	Loyalty	67
	Initiative	68

Chapter 6	**Motivating People**	**69**
	The Two Kinds of Leaders	70
	Understanding the Soul of Your Venture	71
	The Source of Authority	74
	Ownership and Motivation	78
	The Coming Change in Capitalism	80
	The Leadership of Strategic Retreat	81
	Human Ego and the Destruction of Empires	84

Chapter 7	**They Changed the Course of History**	**87**
	The First Battle of Rhodes	88
	Islam in Check	92
	Suleiman Ascends	93
	The Second Battle of Rhodes	94
	The Sultan's Benevolence	96
	The Knights Occupy Malta	97
	The Battle of Malta	98
	The Courage of St. Elmo	99
	No Quarter Will Be Given	101
	Another Miracle	102
	No Retreat	103
	Victory	104
	Europe Celebrates	104
	The Lessons	105
	The Present Status of the Order	106

Chapter 8	**The Five Essentials**	**109**
	The Balance	109
	Managing for Results	110
	Managing a Team	111
	Managing an Army	112
	Managing a Business	113
	Spinning Plates	114
	Simplicity in Diversity	115

Chapter 9   # The Product   **117**

The Moral Importance of the Product   117
Maintaining Our First Love   118
Two Great Leaders   119
Your Product Is You   121
The Foundation of Greatness   121
The Practical Principles of the Product   123

Chapter 10   # Administration—Part I   **127**

Control Growth or Fight Cancer   127
The Overload: Friend or Enemy?   128
The Reward Factor   129
The Chief Executive Officer   130
Tenacity Tempered by Flexibility   130
Two Kinds of Leadership   132
The Aggressor   132
The Conservative   134
The Opportunity of Adversity   136
The Danger of Prosperity   137
The Effective Middle Manager   139
The Test of Faith   140
The Test of Freedom   142

Chapter 11   # Administration—Part II   **145**

The Successful Non-Manager   145
Our Greatest Asset   146
The First Step in Making Leaders   147
Time Management   147
Summary   150

Chapter 12   # Marketing   **153**

Strategic Research   153
Hitting the Target   154
The One for All and All for One Trap   157
Just the Facts Please   158
The Best Promotions   159
Endorsements with Class   159
Honor Your Ambassadors   161
The Essential Skill   161

The Right Start 162
Character Traits of the Golden Salesman 163
Distribution 167

Chapter 13 **Resources** **169**

The Life Is in the Blood 170
Helpful Professionals 170
Common Mistakes 171
The Skill of Investing 175
The Time Value of Money 176
Wisdom with Debt 177
Contrary Investing 178
Dollar Cost Averaging 179
A Warning 181
The Other Side of Debt 182
Positive Collecting 183
Negative Collecting 183
Summary 184

Chapter 14 **Timing** **187**

A Minnow Turns into a Shark 188
The Courage of Patience 189
The Courage of Decisiveness 190
Summary 191

FOREWORD

When I met Rick Joyner several years ago, I knew that he was involved in a number of ministry, education, and business projects, but little did I realize how much influence he would have through this book. I've read many books in my lifetime, and this is definitely one that I recommend for anyone who wants to achieve great things and influence other people.

You see, the world faces a number of challenges as we point toward the year 2000 and beyond, but few are as crucial as the need for men and women who are willing to become leaders. In this book, Rick pinpoints exactly what you and I need to make a difference in our world. From the beginning, he paints a powerful picture of what leadership should be, and the differences between leadership and management. He points out, "Both leadership and management are required for the administration of almost every venture, but they must be recognized as separate, and kept within their own spheres of authority." It's interesting that he also makes it very clear that the qualities that make a person a good leader will often make him a poor manager. Confusion about that one point, I've found, often causes many people with potential to fail.

Building on that foundation, with well-researched stories from history, Rick talks about the vision and the plan—which he calls "The two pillars of leadership." Here is the core of his teaching:

> *Great leaders have seldom taken the mantle of leadership for its own sake. True leadership is born out of vision and strategy that is established firmly on the bedrock of conviction and purpose. Leadership is a means and not the end itself.*

He then points to the underpinnings of those pillars—honor, morality, and character. He writes:

> *Wisdom is the ability to apply knowledge correctly. Courage is the will to apply it. Without wisdom and courage, increased knowledge will only inflict us with "The paralysis of analysis."*

With the strong foundation, the two main pillars and the underpinnings he has established during the first half of the book, Rick then moves into a powerful discussion of the primary needs for success in any enterprise—the product, administration, marketing, resources, and timing.

I don't want to steal Rick's thunder by sharing my thoughts about each of the five essentials. Let me just say that after reading his book, I agree with the process of success he teaches. His writings have confirmed many things that I've believed for a long time.

The breakthrough this book offers is how Rick writes about leadership and success, not with awe—as though great achievers are born that way, but with a passion for teaching how to develop leadership skills.

You will read principles that you can put into practice the same day. You are not asked to become a super-leader overnight, but are encouraged to see the need for long-term growth—which is the true test of leadership.

This book is a "must read." It is written simply, clearly, and practically. In the end, it asks you to challenge many false ideas and to move into a new understanding of the leader you can become.

Rick writes:

> *True leadership and quality management are a lifestyle, not just a course to be understood. This lifestyle requires the continual sharpening of one's skills and knowledge. When that ceases, your leadership, your management, and your life, will almost certainly be in retreat.*

Now the challenge is yours. Will you accept it? You have the information in your hands to touch your world for God, for good, and for greatness. Your dreams are too important to do anything less.

Dexter R. Yager, Sr.
President, *Internet Services Corp.*

Chapter One

The Fundamentals Of Leadership

Leadership is one of the most powerful forces on earth. With it Napoleon, an obscure soldier from Corsica, took a bankrupt and war devastated France and defeated the most powerful nations on earth, dominating Europe during his time. With it a humble lawyer from India, Gandhi, without firing a shot, without holding a political office or military position, broke the strength and will of the greatest empire in the world and gave birth to a nation. With it a pious country gentleman named Robert E. Lee took the hungry and poorly equipped Southern Army during the Civil War, and caused the world to stop and marvel as he won victory after victory against impossible odds.

With this gift, a humble carpenter from the most despised town in the most despised nation on earth, took a dozen of the least likely candidates for leadership—fishermen, malcontents and simple folk who seemed to care little for religion, and with them unleashed the most powerful moral force this world has ever seen. With leadership, this improbable band of ordinary men and women impacted the world for their leader to the degree that the very word "history" came to mean "his-story."

Regardless of one's religious beliefs, the accomplishments of Jesus and his little band are some of the most extraordinary examples of leadership ever produced. Two of this carpenter's followers, Paul and Silas, after suffering numerous stonings, beatings, continuous persecution, and without arms or bands of followers, caused the highest officials of the most powerful empire on earth to cringe with fear when they limped into a city, exclaiming, "Those who have turned the whole world upside down have now come here to us!" When finally captured, this Paul penned a few letters from his prison cell—hardly a significant literary accomplishment, but no other words ever written have impacted the world as much as those brief letters have, now immortalized as canon scripture.

Leadership is a most awesome force to be entrusted to mere men, but because it is, we would do well to understand it. We will either use leadership or be used by it. This issue is fundamental to an understanding of the world and how one fits into it. It affects the lives of everyone every day regardless of whether or not we like it, or understand it. Understanding it can release the ability to live beyond the ordinary and mundane in order to make a difference on this earth.

Leadership combines several characteristics to make one both perceptive and effective in accomplishing his goals. The effective leader will not only have the vision to perceive the future, he will have the wisdom, courage and determination to affect it. One might even be so profound as to say that nothing on this earth has ever been accomplished without leadership—all human advancement is the result of it. Your advancement will depend on the degree to which it resides in you.

LEADERSHIP VS MANAGEMENT

To properly understand leadership we must first distinguish it from management. Confusing management with leadership has caused many an enterprise to fall short of its potential, and in many cases, to fail altogether. This confusion is the cause of much of the failure and recent decline in American economic strength. Both leadership and management are required for the administration of almost every venture, but they must be recognized as separate, and kept within their own spheres of authority.

The qualities that make a good leader will often make one a poor manager. The qualities that make a good manager can hinder one from becoming an effective leader. That is why having good leadership characteristics does not guarantee that one will be a *successful* leader. To be a successful leader one must know how to choose good managers. Not recognizing this need for dependence upon those with different talents has caused some of the most brilliant leaders to briefly excite their world only to fizzle like a burned-out firecracker, having no foundation for lasting success.

Managers must be detail-oriented to be successful; leaders must be concept-oriented, able to see the big picture. Good leaders usually dislike details; good managers may have a hard time seeing beyond them. Of course there are exceptions to this. There are effective managers with leadership ability, and leaders with good management ability. However, the more undistracted devotion we can give to our strongest talents the more effective we will be.

Being too involved with the details makes it hard to see the big picture. When one is focused on the big picture it is likewise hard to see the details effectively. The most effective leadership comes from a partnership of those who lead and those who manage, a partnership that allows each to concentrate on his own role.

Almost every great enterprise has been founded by a leader, not a manager. Even so, almost every enterprise that lives past its founder is then taken over by a manager. There are two basic reasons for this: 1) There are so few leaders who can make it through the gauntlet of the hierarchy, and 2) Most leaders are poor managers and fail to understand the need for a partnership with managers; therefore the enterprise will be in desperate need of a manager at the top for awhile.

When the manager first takes over, profitability and efficiency will usually increase for a period of time, but progress under the manager type will invariably slow, jeopardizing future success. Then the organization will usually swing back to a leader-type for its next head. Most organizations, from corporations to churches, that have existed for a period of time, will constantly switch from manager-type to leader-type at the top.

THE GAUNTLET

The advancement system in a typical hierarchy, which is the structure of almost every human enterprise, makes it hard for one with good leadership qualities to rise to a position of leadership. The lower echelons of a hierarchy usually reward management skills more than those of leadership. A leader will rarely be good enough at the managerial skills required for advancement within the system—unless he devotes himself to the quality that will be most needed when he does come to his place of leadership—*discipline*.

The detail-oriented management skills so foreign to his nature, must be understood by the leader if he is to effectively work with those whose work will be essential to his success as a leader. The typical hierarchy will be most difficult for even a great leader to advance in, but those who do advance will be those best prepared for their task. Even if it is tedious and boring, the potential leader should see the hierarchy as his cocoon. It is the great struggle required by the butterfly to get out of its cocoon that strengthens it so that it can use those great wings. It will likewise be the potential leader's struggle to get to the top of the hierarchy which prepares him for the great responsibility of leadership.

THE ESSENTIAL PARTNERSHIP

Advancement requires seeing beyond the present limits of our time, a realm where the true leader abides, but where the manager has difficulty. A manager looks at what *is*; a leader is always looking for what *can be*. It takes both qualities to get the full picture; either one without the other is ultimately doomed to mediocrity or failure. If the managers understood leadership, and the leaders understood management, there would almost certainly be far less decline in enterprise, and both leadership and management would be more effective.

The leader's job is to give the managers direction, vision and inspiration. Regardless of how good the leader is, he will be ineffective without good managers. His degree of success or failure will be determined by the quality of managers he can recruit. Discerning the quality and ability of his people and using them properly is just as important in accomplishing goals as having the vision and other resources required for the enterprise.

General Robert E. Lee was one of the great military leaders of all time. General "Stonewall" Jackson was one of the great military managers of all time. As *a team* they may have been as close to being invincible as any two generals ever came. It was a simple coalition; Lee would determine what needed to be done, Jackson would determine how to do it.

Either of these celebrated generals without the other would probably have never risen to the heights of accomplishment that they were able to attain as a team. Lee could not have been as great a leader without Jackson to take the burden of management. With Jackson, Lee could concentrate on that at which he was best—seeing the overall picture. Without Lee, Jackson's abilities to implement strategies may have gone unnoticed or under used. These two made each other great and gave the other the opportunity to realize his full potential. Such teams are rare, but they would probably be more common if we just had the insight to see and give opportunity to the qualities and potential of our co-workers.

Lee was also a very good military manager, and Jackson was certainly an outstanding leader. These abilities are not always mutually exclusive, but most leaders who have achieved success did so with the support of talented managers who enabled them to concentrate on the big picture. Although exceptions to this are rare, two of the most notable ones in history remarkably lived during the same period, and actually confronted each other in one of the great epic military battles of all time—Napoleon and Wellington who faced each other at The Battle of Waterloo.

Napoleon was a colossus, the type of leader who has only emerged every few hundred years. He was not only a great military genius, he was also a great political genius. It was this combination that enabled him to dominate the age in which he lived, and to a large degree, set the course of history since his time. Some of his military innovations would provide a foundation for modern military strategy. Some of his political innovations have done the same for government and law.

MANAGEMENT BASED LEADERSHIP

Napoleon's genius for military strategy was actually born of his genius for military management. Likewise, his genius for political leadership was born of his genius for political management. Napoleon is a study of how this rare combination of great leadership and great management in one person can carry him to the very limits of human potential. The few leaders who have been so gifted have dominated almost every great historic period.

Napoleon's innovative military strategies were based on the maneuverability of his forces. This maneuverability was based upon his management strategies, which streamlined the method of supplying the troops. This opened strategic possibilities for Napoleon that the opposing forces did not even have the option of considering. Because of this he could quickly overwhelm a superior force, and at times, use a single army to rout several others at once.

Except for Wellington, it could be argued that Napoleon had no peer in history on the field of battle. But Wellington was not only his peer, he was both a better military leader *and* manager than Napoleon. Possibly the only man in history who could stop Napoleon on the battlefield was the one who did stop him. The odds against two men as remarkable as Napoleon and Wellington living during the same period, much less actually confronting one another in battle, would defy computation. The battle itself, Waterloo, met or surpassed any expectations of the genius in management and power of leadership that these two would focus upon each other.

Wellington was a British officer who began his military career in India. He gained some notoriety by winning battles and subduing forts with intelligence and innovation, but he did not gain much respect due to the low regard the public had for his adversaries. Through a remarkable set of circumstances he was transferred and given command of The Peninsula Campaign in Portugal and Spain. While the depressed allies expected little out of this campaign, Wellington surprised the world by liberating Portugal and Spain while defeating some of Napoleon's top generals and troops.

Wellington's victories, combined with Napoleon's debacle in Russia, sent Napoleon into exile. With the armies disbanded Wellington returned to Britain. Early the next year Napoleon returned to France, quickly gathered his loyal troops and marched on Brussels. Wellington was dispatched to command a quickly assembled allied army, comprised of diverse troops with different languages and bickering generals who were in some cases political appointees with little military ability. Few of his lieutenants understood Wellington's newly devised strategies. The British general's task looked impossible. His battlefield problems appeared stupendous, and he was even significantly outnumbered.

PEACE OF MIND—THE FOUNDATION FOR VICTORY

Wellington's calm in the storm of battle had already become legendary. On one occasion, after giving orders that he felt would accomplish the victory, he was seen catching a quick snooze right on the field of battle. The night before Waterloo he actually attended a ball. A number of his victories were directly attributed to his personal entry into the thickest part of the battle to rally his troops, and was never seen to flinch even as men fell all around him. Wellington acknowledged that his peace in the midst of such conflict was supernatural, a gift from above. At Waterloo supernatural leadership, and supernatural management would both be required of him.

Just south of Brussels, one hundred and fifty thousand men faced each other in less than three square miles of territory. Napoleon had nothing but contempt for "the sepoy general" he faced that day; he seemed almost bored with the looming battle, and was looking forward to dining in Brussels that evening.

ARROGANCE—THE FOUNDATION FOR DEFEAT

Besides scorn for his adversary's ability, Napoleon knew he had significant numerical advantages in troops and guns. He even slept late, almost casually arrayed his troops and did not begin the battle until after eleven o'clock. This poor timing was possibly the only strategic mistake Napoleon was to make that day, but it was all that Wellington would need.

A biblical proverb states, "Pride comes before the fall," and that explains the downfall of many of history's great leaders. Napoleon at Waterloo gives one of history's most resounding punctuations to that truth. Previous successes can be the seed of ultimate destruction if they produce arrogance.

With the sun already high, Napoleon ordered his artillery to begin one of the greatest cannonades ever witnessed. Then a huge thunderstorm broke upon the field that actually drowned out the cannonade, disconcerting the French. (This thunderstorm phenomenon had accompanied some of Wellington's most important victories; he testified that it was "the finger of God.") The deluge so softened the field that the cannon balls lost some of their deadly potential as the ground just absorbed them. The mud also reduced Napoleon's maneuverability. This was just the beginning of a score of "miracles" Wellington would need, and receive, that day. But it was not *just* the miracles that saved him; he was a man who was prepared to brilliantly seize and derive every drop of help that he could from each one.

CRISIS—THE COCOON OF THE GREAT

All day long the wounded and routed allied soldiers poured into Brussels. Every new group gave the same report—Wellington was beaten and the French were just behind them. Actually their reports were understandable. At any time during the day one could have looked at the allied position and determined that it was hopeless. One general later reported, "From noon until the very last moment of the battle, it was one continuous crisis."

It was under just such pressure that Wellington excelled. He seemed to be omnipresent. He was always at the point of the greatest crisis, directing and rallying his men. He kept the big picture of the overall battle while he also personally directed individual regiments. He kept track of every "pawn" in this most deadly chess match. He seemed to always appear just in time, with just enough men, with just enough resolve, to barely escape disaster. After plugging one hole he would gallop off to the other end of the field where he suspected another emergency, and he would usually find it as expected. A lesser man would have retreated or surrendered a dozen times that day. Napoleon brilliantly pressed every advantage, but was repeatedly stopped by the narrowest of margins.

By mid-afternoon Napoleon began to suspect that "the sepoy general" had some ability. That morning Napoleon had told his staff that the odds were ten to one that they would be in Brussels by nightfall. By afternoon he acknowledged to those gathered around him that the odds were now only six to four.

Finally Napoleon's General Ney overwhelmed the out-numbered allies to take strategic ground in the center of Wellington's position. This was the most feared disaster for the allies. Napoleon astutely followed up this advantage with what would certainly be the death blow—he sent his famous Old Guard into the gaping hole in Wellington's center.

In their many battles, the Guard had never been repulsed. Both armies stood in awe at their massive assault in parade formations across the field. Wellington may have been the only one on the entire field who gave himself a chance at that point. Amazingly, he was observed as confident and calm as ever. A cannon shot sailed over the neck of his horse and cleanly severed the leg of his second in command. Wellington simply reached over and shook the general's hand, expressing his condolences, and galloped off to another vantage point.

As the Guard approached Wellington's center, he waved his hand and a regiment rose from behind a stone wall to pour a deadly volley into the French. Then out of a cornfield emerged Colonel Colborne's regiment. Colborne's general galloped up to him to ask his intentions. Colborne stated simply, "I'm going to make that column feel my fire." At that moment Wellington's aide arrived with the order for Colborne to advance from the cornfield.

All day long Wellington had remarkably kept in his mind the position of every brigade and regiment. In spite of the multitude of crises in which he could have desperately used this regiment, he resisted until the *perfect* time.

The battle for the center became a caldron of death. The Old Guard felt Colborne's fire and they faltered. At this point Colborne heard a voice beside him saying, "Go ahead, press them. You're doing it, press them now." The colonel turned to see who was speaking and was astonished to find Wellington himself.

The entire French army groaned as they beheld a sight they had never witnessed before—the Guard's perfect formations disintegrating as they fled from their positions in disarray. After being pressed to the limits all day, Wellington's most desperate crisis quickly became his one brief opportunity for victory—and he seized it. He poured his few remaining reserves into the fray, and at the right time the Belgian division arrived.

Moments before the situation had appeared utterly hopeless, and now the entire French army began to collapse. The Guard's reserves formed squares and took their stand to protect the retreat. After they were surrounded, and were asked to surrender, their reply was to the point: "The Old Guard dies, but it never surrenders." They died, and Napoleon's power over Europe died with them.

As darkness fell fifty thousand men lay upon the field. Over a dozen men had attended Wellington that morning; that evening he dined with his one remaining aide. He felt no elation in the victory. In keeping with his notorious understatements concerning his own accomplishments, he simply claimed to have done what anyone else would have done in his place. This tendency was never given or perceived as a false modesty; Wellington was a remarkably humble man. If he ever succumbed to overstatement it was in relation to his shortcomings, not his accomplishments. The truly great do not have to blow their own trumpets—others will do it for them.

Napoleon was defeated by his own arrogance. Wellington was confident but never arrogant. There is a difference which every truly great leader has understood. Effective confidence is founded in a humility that produces a right perspective of his circumstances. Wellington's belief in his appointed destiny gave him the ability to keep peace of mind under the greatest of pressures. It is possible that no other man in history ever faced such pressure from crisis after crisis within a single day, with so much at stake, and performed so brilliantly. Even the smallest mistake, or slightest hesitance in reacting to any single one of the crises, could have meant doom, for his army and possibly the entire continent of Europe.

The real test of leadership always comes in crisis, and there will be crisis for everyone in leadership. Almost every businessman will sooner or later have to make decisions that can mean life or death to his business. Often, the more successful the businessman, the more frequent such decisions will have to be made. The greater the potential for success inherent in the decision, the greater the potential for failure it will likewise carry.

Every coach will have to call plays that mean victory or defeat. The more successful the coach, the more such calls he will have to make, and the higher the stakes will be. It may not be too difficult to make the proper decision or to call the right play when there is little on the line; the difference between the great ones and the rest is the ability to do it in the crisis when there is more at risk.

DEFEAT—THE FOUNDATION FOR FUTURE VICTORY

I once built a successful business in a short period of time. To build it as rapidly as I did I had to make dozens of decisions that could have meant life or death to the enterprise. I made a few right decisions that paid great dividends. I then made just one bad decision, and that single mistake ultimately led to the bankruptcy of the entire business. It was a painful, humiliating failure, but I consider it one of my most valuable experiences. I learned more from that one defeat than from all of my victories combined. This is not to imply that I did not make other mistakes but this was one of truly critical significance.

The baseball player who stands at the plate with the potential for being the hero, can also be the goat. Just as Wellington turned the biggest reversal of the day into his chance for victory; we must maintain the same resolve. If you will keep your patience and peace of mind in the midst of crisis, you will usually see an opportunity to use the situation to your advantage.

The 1980's saw the amazing rise of the Christian *mega ministries*. It was no surprise that such ministries which grew so fast would stay in a perpetual state of crisis, tottering between oblivion and extraordinary advancement. After overcoming a multitude of life and death struggles, some of the biggest and most successful of these ministries began to unravel because of just one major mistake by their leaders. The lessons abound that one moment of weakness and poor judgment is able to undo many years of labor built upon good judgement and effective leadership in crisis.

With success comes power, and power inevitably brings a subtle corruption of our judgement, a seeming invincibility that is often the fatal delusion. One of most important ingredients in Wellington's character was his ability to have confidence while not thinking more highly of himself than he should. In his letters penned from prison, the apostle Paul gave a most appropriate warning to those in leadership, "When you think you stand, take heed lest you fall." This illusion of invincibility could be called *The Titanic Syndrome.*

Chapter Two

The Titanic Syndrome

When built, the Titanic was a symbol of the opulence and sense of invincibility the British Empire felt in those days. She reflected that period's extravagance, and arrogance, as well as the belief that nothing could sink its expanding world economy and dominion. Few at that time dreamed that in just two years the world would be at war, and that their invincible empire was about to hit an iceberg that would ultimately send it to the same end as all of man's previous empires. The world's wealthy and famous streamed onto the Titanic for the maiden voyage. Because they didn't think she could sink they sailed boldly into dangerous waters with reckless abandon. This "unsinkable" pride of the Empire proved to be incredibly fragile—just as the Empire was, as is every empire. Arrogance can be the greatest weakness of all.

In relation to the present world economy it has been repeated often, and believed by most, that what happened in 1929 could never happen again. Experts say there are too many safeguards—a stronger Federal Reserve, higher margin requirements for speculators and institutions, FDIC, FSLIC, SIPC, etc... Do not believe it for a minute! We are now more vulnerable to a worldwide economic catastrophe than at any time in history, and we are merrily sailing along in the most treacherous of seas.

In 1929 U.S. corporations had $1.54 in cash for every $1.00 of debt. Presently they have less than 15 cents in cash for each dollar of debt. If we start measuring individual and third world debt, not to mention the huge federal deficit, the economic icebergs in our path begin to seem completely impassable. The Fed, FDIC and all the other safeguards are lifeboats that may save a few, but they are wholly inadequate for the voyage we're on. The owners of the Titanic felt that having even half the lifeboats a ship her size should have carried was superfluous; after all, she was unsinkable! Today's leaders are sailing with the same disdain for reason while touting their ingenuity in designing a ship they think cannot sink. We must not let the euphoria of the apparent collapsing of communism cause us to utterly succumb to the terrible delusion already gripping us.

Democracy is the most just and benevolent form of government devised by man, but it is by no means the most efficient. Its nature makes it difficult for leaders to face problems until they have become a crisis. Because of the process required to get elected in a democracy, those who are best qualified to either lead or manage seldom get involved. Historically we have been blessed with just enough leadership, just in time to save us from oblivion when crisis exploded upon us. The present financial crisis has the potential of being the most deadly we have ever confronted.

When the Titanic hit the iceberg there was a disconcerting jolt. Just about everyone noticed it, but after a few minutes the party continued. From the captain to the last third class passenger, no one imagined that in just a couple of hours most of them would be on the bottom. The ship was so big and warm, and all of the "experts" said it was unsinkable. It was not the iceberg that sank the Titanic—it was *COMPLACENCY*.

Wise and decisive Leadership could have prevented the disaster; perhaps it can still save us.

Historians marvel at the repetitious cycles of human error. Few have been able to break out of these cycles. Few have been wise enough to see anything but what they wanted to see in the trends and events taking place around them. Those in authority, by the nature of their power, feel compelled to put the best face on problems. Only the most courageous leaders have been able to hear the warnings and take action. Empire after empire, nation after nation, companies, organizations, churches, and families, continue to fail because their leaders refuse to face problems until they are beyond control.

Roger Smith, the former Chairman of General Motors, stated after the October 19, 1987 Stock Market crash, "We didn't just have a tummy ache here in our country; we had a genuine, certified heart attack! If you don't recognize it as a heart attack, and if you don't get on that diet and start doing your exercise, you can have another one and it could be terminal."

In many ways the economy parallels the operation of an engine, which is why it is often referred to as one. As a jet pilot one of the first things I learned was to pay attention to my engine instruments and know what they were telling me. Even if the particular systems were staying within their tolerances, certain trends could foretell serious problems. If there are erratic oscillations, even though they stay within given parameters, the engine may not just quit, it could very well explode! The economic instruments of the entire world are not only oscillating wildly, but they have long ago and by a large margin, departed safe parameters.

The degree of complacency of the leadership on the Titanic was incomprehensible and clearly the reason for the disaster. Captain Smith and his crew received numerous warnings about the ice field which lay directly across their path—and they did not even slow down! Even if she were unsinkable, to hit an iceberg head on would cause great damage and probably loss of life. But Smith ignored the danger while maintaining an incredible false sense of security. When looking at the course of Western economic policy for the last few decades the parallels are striking. What could our leaders possibly be thinking?

The Titanic's crew had never held a proper lifeboat drill. They did not have a plan for the orderly movement of passengers to the boats, and most of the crew did not even know how to lower them. Everything had to be planned and learned while the ship was sinking under their feet. This obviously contributed to a much greater loss of life than was necessary. Many boats were lowered only partially filled, one with just twelve people, while hundreds of passengers were held below deck by the crew. The entire ship had been caught off guard by the events of that fateful night, and they paid dearly for it. Will we be caught in the same position? If we are we will pay just as dearly. The ability to cope with crisis is necessary for anyone in leadership, but an even higher goal is to have enough wisdom to take action *before* the situation reaches a crisis. How many of our crises are unnecessary and are actually the result of poor leadership?

There were two other ships which played a significant role in the drama of the Titanic disaster: the Californian and the Carpathia. The captains of these ships, along with Smith of the Titanic, reflect some of the best and the worst characteristics of leadership.

The Californian had a reserved and cautious captain. When he heard about the ice in his path, he slowed down. When he saw the ice he ordered the ship stopped and waited for daylight. His wireless (radio) operator began warning the other ships in the area of the danger. At 7:30 p.m. her warning was received and logged by the Titanic.

This was one of six warnings the Titanic received that evening, all of which were disregarded. This, as much as anything, tells the story of the indifference which permeated her bridge. It was not just the captain, but the entire bridge staff who received and paid little or no attention to the warnings. When this attitude overcomes the leadership, doom is imminent.

The usually stormy North Atlantic was amazingly calm that night. More than one officer said they had never seen the sea so tranquil. First officer Lightoller of the Titanic made this observation at the inquiry when he declared that "everything was against us."

The tranquility of the sea must have also overcome the crew of the Californian. Her bridge watch saw the Titanic approaching just a few miles away; then they saw her stop dead in the water. At first they thought she was taking the same precautions for the ice which they had taken. The captain told the watch to wake him if there were any developments. Then the Titanic fired a rocket, which is always a distress signal at sea. When awakened the captain reasoned that she must be signaling another company ship which they could not see. The wireless operator was asleep and they did not even wake him to see if he could contact the Titanic. Then more rockets were fired as the Californian's crew continued to delude themselves with the same explanation. They actually watched the Titanic go down, telling each other as her lights dimmed and slipped beneath the sea that she was sailing away! Had they responded to the first distress signal the Californian may well have been able to save all of those who perished.

The complacency on the Titanic and the Californian may seem beyond belief, but will the present political and economic leadership look any less frozen in their stupor to the next generation? When the final inquiry comes and the story is told, are we going to be facing the same judgment? Will the band keep playing for us while we slip beneath the sea? Rationalization is a popular shield for cowards, while those with the courage to proclaim the warning are dubbed "alarmists," and their message negativism.

The other ship in the fateful drama of the Titanic was the Carpathia, captained by Arthur H. Rostron. He was known for his ability to make quick decisions and to energize those who served under him. He was a pious man devoted to prayer. At 12:35 a.m. the Carpathia's wireless operator burst into Rostron's quarters to report that the Titanic had struck an iceberg. Rostron reacted in character—he immediately ordered the Carpathia to turn around and accelerate to full speed in the direction of the Titanic; then he asked the wireless operator if he were sure of the message! This showed a remarkable contrast to the reaction of the California crew.

Rostron then gave a powerful demonstration of truly prepared leadership—he thought of everything. He ordered the English doctor to the first class dining room, the Italian doctor to second class, the Hungarian to third class, along with every possible piece of equipment or supplies needed for sick or wounded. He ordered different officers to different gangways, instructing them to get the names of survivors to send by wireless. They prepared block and lines with chair slings for the wounded. Bowlines were secured along the sides of the ship, with boat ropes and heaving lines, for securing the lifeboats. All gangway doors were opened. He then directed specific officers to be in charge of his present passengers, to take care of their needs and keep them out of the way. All hands were ordered to prepare coffee, soup and provisions. He then designated the officer's cabins, smoke rooms, library, etc., to accommodate the survivors. Stewards were sent to reassure and explain the activity to their own passengers.

Then Rostron turned to face the biggest problem of all—the ice. He was heading at full speed into the same field that had stopped the Titanic. To him reducing speed was out of the question, but he took every measure to reduce the risk to his own ship and passengers. He added a man to the crow's nest, put two more on the bow, one on each wing of the bridge, and he stayed there himself. His second officer, James Bisset, then noticed the captain taking one last measure which he considered the most important of all—he prayed.

At 2:45 a.m. Bisset saw the first iceberg. They steered around it and kept going. During the next hour they dodged five more. At 4:00 a.m. they reached the Titanic's last called position and began picking up lifeboats. As the sun rose it revealed a sight they would never forget—the sea was full of icebergs for as far as the eye could see. Even with all the lookouts, the Carpathia had passed numerous ones which they had not even seen.

The difficult rescue of the Titanic's survivors was carried out with such order that peace reigned over all. The Carpathia's passengers caught the spirit of self-sacrifice from the crew. Her first class passengers gave their own quarters to survivors; others did all they could. On one of the darkest nights of tragedy ever experienced on the high seas, the Carpathia's captain, crew and passengers stand out as bright lights of courage and heroism. They are a demonstration of what true leadership is all about. They did not sleep as others did, and were not fooled by the calmness of the sea—they were PREPARED and they took action.

Chapter Three

You Are Here

A friend of mine, Dr. Jack Deere, once told of a small incident that became very meaningful to him. He had gone to a large shopping mall to meet some friends at a designated place. He entered the mall and went to the large map showing the layout of the stores. When he found the place where he was supposed to meet his friends, he took off in a direction that turned out to be wrong, because he had failed to first find the dot that says *you are here.*

By its very definition, leadership must be going somewhere, but before we take off too fast, we must know where we are going and where we are starting from. This chapter is an attempt to show, in a general sense from the perspective of history, the blue dot that tells us where we are.

THE FOUR GREAT EPOCHS OF HISTORY

There have been four great epochs of human history. Each was dominated by a different "power base," which gave definition to that era. These power bases were: MILITARY, RELIGION, POLITICS, and ECONOMICS. Understanding, and using, these power bases is the foundation upon which the leadership of the world has been based.

For example, the period preceding the advent of Christ was dominated by Military power. This was the age of the conquerors. Christianity became the first Religion to actually rival the Military power base for influencing world affairs. By the forth century A.D., the Roman Emperor Constantine rightly discerned that the power base of Religion would actually eclipse the Military power base in influence. Like the popular proverb, perceiving that he could not beat it, he joined it. (In the context of this chapter, the "Religious power base" is related to the institutions of Religion as distinguished from personal religious faith).

From the fourth century until the Renaissance, the Religious power base ascended to dominate world affairs, with institutional Christianity rising in the West and Islam in the East. During this time the Military power was used as a tool for exerting religious dominance. Both Politics and Economics were being developed, and gained influence during this time, but were mostly used to serve the Religious power base.

As Politics began to emerge as a main source of influence in the sixteenth century, governments were invented and developed, while the institution of feudalism lost its power. Then the Military and Religious power bases became extensions of the Political powers. Economics, which had been ascending in power for several centuries, began to emerge as the main source of influence during the twentieth century. With the polarities of communism and capitalism vying for the dominant role in this new power base, the Military, Religious and Political power bases have all, to a degree, become extensions of the Economic powers.

History is not quite as clean and fluid as the above might infer, but in a general sense, we can see that these four great power bases are the four major influences dominating the course of civilization. In different regions there were periods when the Military power base would reassert its influence, and become dominant for a short period during the time of the Religious, Political or Economic eras. We can also see the Religious power base reasserting itself as the primary source of influence during the epochs of the other power bases, such as the Great Awakenings in the eighteenth and nineteenth centuries, and the recent Islamic fundamentalist revolution in Iran. In the former Soviet Union we now have an interesting clash of the Political, Economic and Military power bases all seeking a dominant role, with the Religious influence also growing dramatically through a grassroots movement.

A FOUNDATION FOR UNDERSTANDING THE FUTURE

Understanding these four primary sources of power that affect foundational shifts in civilization can provide a paradigm for understanding the general flow of the past, the present, and the future. A paradigm is a model that we use for perceiving, understanding and interpreting the world. It is useless to know what happened in history if we do not understand it, and are not able to apply that understanding to affect our future. However, if we are going to fully understand where we are headed, and why, we must also have a solid foundation of understanding where we have been. It is no accident that almost all of the great leaders of history were also devoted students of history with a powerful historic perspective.

Clausewitz was a German officer during the Napoleonic wars and his book, *On War* interpreted the place of the Military power base in much the same way that Machiavelli's book, *The Prince*, had interpreted the Political power base. Clausewitz defined war as the attempt of one nation to extend its Political will over another. In Clausewitz' time war truly was an extension of Politics, because he wrote during the nineteenth century when the Political power base was dominant. However, if he were writing his classic book today he would almost certainly declare that wars are basically extensions of Economic interests.

To understand the world today, we must understand that all of the other power bases are serving the dominant power base of Economics. This is not a statement of what is right or wrong, but simply what is fact.

UNDERSTANDING ECONOMIC WAR

As the world has been moving deeper into the period dominated by the Economic power base, it is clear that most of the world-changing conflicts are Economic in nature. The Cold War was a very real war, but it was an Economic war, not a Military war. The great clash between communism and capitalism was an Economic clash more than it was a Political clash. The former Soviet Union was beaten Economically, not Militarily. Religious power struggles often degenerated into Military wars during the Middle Ages, and this could have happened during the Cold War, but by the grace of God it did not. Even so, the Political and Economic changes that were accomplished by the Cold War were as sweeping and deep as have ever been accomplished during a Military war, including World War II.

The 1992 monetary crisis in Europe was the Economic equivalent of a significant military battle, but this battle was fought with banks, currencies, and computers instead of infantry, artillery and air forces. The long term effect of that monetary conflict promises to be as far reaching in its impact on the course of Europe as many of the great military battles fought between those same nations.

It has been said often that the United States won the war against Japan but Japan has been winning the peace. The fact is that what we have been considering "peace" has been a very real war with every bit as much strategic significance as the World War fought with armies and navies. The United States did win the Military war but Japan has been winning the Economic war, a war that has the power to bring both Political,

Economic and even Religious changes every bit as profound as World War II.

Understanding the present nature of this conflict is crucial for any nation that expects to field a successful "army" during this period. The most important "generals" in the present world war are corporate presidents, bankers and other economic leaders. The most important army is now composed of workers, small business owners, accountants and other business oriented professionals. Computers are now more powerful than bombs and bullets. Economic spying is now emphasized more than military spying. (It is interesting to note that the Soviets actually considered the I.R.S. as the true counterparts of the K.G.B.).

Economics is now the most powerful force dictating political changes. Even though George Bush lead the United States in one of the most decisive military victories in history, presided over the consummating victory of the Cold War, and for a time reached unprecedented heights of popularity, Bill Clinton soundly thrashed him in the next election by discerning and using this great power shift. Clinton recognized that the Economic power base is now more powerful than Military, Religious, or Political influences, so he built his platform where the real power was. Bush's popularity as a president began to fade when the public began to recognize that he did not understand, or emphasize, Economic leadership as the most important kind of leadership that the president must now have.

A NEW BREED OF LEADER

Already, any nation's ability to lead in world affairs in relation to Military, Religious or Political issues depends on her Economic strength. Many of the general principles of leadership are the same for any type of leader—Military, Religious, Political, or little league coaching. However, with the transition of each power base to a new one, some of the rules of leadership have changed as well. With the transition to each new dominant power base, the stakes for leadership have also risen dramatically. That is, the decisions made by leadership will affect many more people, more quickly. It is now more obvious than ever that if good leadership does not emerge to confront the basic issues of our time, the most diabolical forces will quickly fill the vacuum to control our future.

In the late 1980's we witnessed the astonishingly swift collapse of the most powerful communist empires. As stated, it was not Military power that caused this collapse, but Economic power. This resulted in one of the most profound political power shifts in history—and it was accomplished in just a few short weeks! Never in the history of the world was there such a cataclysmic power shift in such a short period of time. With the change in each of the power bases as the primary force in world affairs, the rate of civilization-wide changes has also greatly accelerated. The new leadership must be able to assimilate knowledge and act on it much faster than has been previously required. To be a leader in the world today requires much more than just knowing where we have been, or even where we are today—world leadership today requires prophetic insight into where we are going, with the wisdom and will to act on future probabilities as if they were historic facts.

The skills required of today's leaders are also different. For example, an important knowledge or skill for a leader during the Military epoch was to understand how men react in extreme danger, and knowing how to control them in that situation. He also would need to understand the different weapons and their most effective deployment. During the Religious epoch, perceiving and controlling men's fears and hopes was the knowledge of power. In the Political epoch, cultural knowledge, and the ability to write or make motivating speeches would have been more important for world leadership. In this Economic age, the ability to find and use information quickly and properly, is an essential skill for anyone trying to lead. Information can now be more powerful than armies, and is now the most valuable commodity in the world, when measured in the percentage of people, time, and other resources devoted to it.

THE PRICE OF CHANGE

The ability to anticipate and quickly adjust to change is essential for survival in today's circles of power. This is especially true in democracies where the government is still run by Political leaders who are ignorant of, and insensitive to, Economic power. This may come as a surprise when we think that democracies tend to be the most capitalistic, and won the economic cold war against communism. However, even though capitalism may have outlasted communism, it is also tottering on the brink of changes that promise to be as radical as those experienced by the communist states. Much of Western capitalism's ability to outlast communism was its ability to borrow more for longer periods of time. This foundation of debt is not a very solid foundation, and huge cracks can already be seen in it. The bill will soon come due, and the inability of our political leaders to understand the impending economic catastrophe promises to make it even more painful than it would have had to be.

This does not mean that we will return to communism, but there are other alternatives. The refusal of the Religious leaders with their Middle Age mentality to release their authority to the emerging Political power base, made the price of change much higher than was necessary in terms of human lives and the destruction of Religious influence. The similar reluctance of the Political leaders to relinquish control in the Economic areas where they lack the wisdom to lead effectively, is likewise promising to force a most destructive transition.

For example, the constant changing of the tax rules has created a business environment similar to playing a game when the rules are being constantly changed, but no one tells you until after the fact. As soon as you develop a strategy according to one set of rules, they are changed, which not only makes your strategy obsolete, it also leaves you in a position that is the opposite of where you need to be.

A striking example of this involved the Tax Reform Bill passed by the Reagan Administration. Even a cursory look at this bill should have alerted anyone that the Savings & Loan industry was doomed to losses that they could not absorb. A large percentage of the commercial real estate development that the S&L's had financed was made because of the existing tax laws. It is true that these rules may have created artificial value in this market, but investors were simply playing according to the rules, which they had no idea would be changed in the middle of the game. When the rules were changed, property values plummeted, throwing many S&L's, investors, and other large businesses into insolvency.

In fairness to the Reagan Administration, the Tax Reforms were badly needed to address some areas of economic unfairness, and even economic insanity that was stimulated by unrealistic tax codes. However, there was a need for much more insight and patience than was used. Had the changes been instituted over a period of time, maybe five to ten years. Businesses could have adjusted their strategies and compensated for them without the devastating losses that the whole country ultimately had to pay, of which the S&L debacle was just a portion.

The Reagan Tax Reform had a ripple effect throughout the entire economy from which it will take years to recover. A major negative impact was caused by a loss of faith in the rules. Many who want to play in the economic game by starting new businesses, or making investments, now find it hard to make the kind of long term plans that solid, lasting economic development requires. This kind of impact cannot be measured on graphs, but it is easy to observe the dramatic effect in the way many now do business—and this is unquestionably a negative effect.

The government, apparently trying to cover up its tragic mistake, paraded a few of the S&L crooks as an example to the nation of how these evil men had destroyed an industry. There are such crooks in every industry, but they were by no means the reason for the S&L collapse. This was just another example of the government, made up of politicians, not really understanding the consequences of their actions in this Economic Age.

Farm subsidies are likewise doing to farmers what was done to many commercial real estate investors. Many of the subsidies and programs are seriously outdated, and need to be changed, but this must be done with careful planning over a period of time, or it will needlessly doom many farmers.

GOD SAVE DEMOCRACY

Because of the historically proven nature of man, democracy is the best form of government on earth. However, we must also recognize that it is the most inefficient. Even so, there are some factors that are more important than efficiency, such as liberty. But to survive, democracy must make some changes. If we allow democracy to make the needed changes to conform to the times, it will become better, not worse. If it does not make these changes it will be doomed, which would be one of the great tragedies of civilization.

Presently, with but a few exceptions, governments are usually the greatest obstacle to solid, sensible economic development. This conflict is seldom intended, but even when the government tries to help business the results are often counterproductive. When the rules of the business game are changed with each new election, and sometimes even more frequently, it is impossible for business to form and stick to the kind of strategies that are necessary for a solid, lasting advance, based on true productivity and not just debt. It is the proper place of government to provide a "level playing field," but it is not right for it to keep changing the rules in the middle of the game.

I have met many of the great business and political leaders in this country. I can usually recognize true leadership gifts very quickly, and many of the greatest leaders today are in business. However, few businessmen will become involved in government because the process of election is so foreign, and distasteful, to their temperament. Our legislative bodies are composed mostly of lawyers, few of whom understand much about business. Only a businessman is going to really understand business, and presently they are almost shut out of the real circles of power in the system. If this does not change in America, we will not only be in jeopardy of losing our leadership in the future, we may not even have a seat from which to watch it.

Democracies have proven incapable of making radical changes until forced to by a crisis. We are headed for such a crisis, and those who are wise know it, and are planning for it. The economic crisis that is looming will either thrust us to a new level of civilization, or an unprecedented level of both tyranny and anarchy.

A NEW DEMOCRACY

We must also add to this equation the fact that democracy is not only inefficient, but also the slowest form of government. Being utterly committed to the fact that democracy is the only safe form of government, it is time to examine ways to speed up the democratic process if it is going to survive. The means and technology do exist to do this, and it would greatly enhance the ability of citizens to participate in the process of government.

The national "town meeting" format, pioneered by the news media and used by candidates in the last election, is an interesting development. With the present technology available, "grassroots democracy," where referendums that involve all citizens are used to make major governmental decisions, could soon be a reality. The stock markets already operate on this principle. Every stock transaction is somebody's positive or negative vote on a company. This is the way Economic authority is now exercised. Every weekday several hundred million such "votes" are processed and posted almost immediately. If they can do this why can't the government?

There has been some progress made in this direction. In the past, if a president wanted to pass certain legislation it had to be worked out with the congress. Now, with television and other almost instant media, they go straight to the people, and have the people write or call their representatives. But why not cut out the extra, expensive step and let the people vote after they have heard the debate?

The main reason this is not being proposed is because those in power would lose much of their power, but that change will come if democracy is to survive. In the past, democratic representatives were chosen because the people were too involved with survival, and many simply did not have the education or time to analyze the issues, so they chose those who they thought could best do it for them. With the advent of modern communications media, now almost every citizen is more educated about every issue than the representatives were just a few decades ago. There will always be the need for representatives, but their job will probably gravitate toward doing what the committees are now doing—choosing and wording the laws that are to be voted on.

If the Political power base does not keep up with the changes being instituted by the Economic power base, its very existence as a real power will be threatened. The alternatives will range from the tyranny of despots to the chilling biblical prophesies of the sub-human "beast," which takes over the whole earth with its ability to control the "buying, selling and trading."

The alternatives

During times of economic crisis men usually look to tyrants because they can work economic "miracles." Hitler took over a bankrupt and war devastated Germany in the 30's, with almost 50% unemployment and a debt and deficit that in today's value greatly exceeds that of any present Western nation. In just four years he not only balanced the budget, but paid off the entire debt! He also restored full employment, and a level of productivity that was unprecedented in human history. His economic accomplishments were nothing less than supernatural.

Hitler's social accomplishments were no less remarkable than his economic miracle. He almost entirely eradicated crime and perversion—except the crime and perversion that he instituted against the Jews. Tyranny can accomplish great things, but is it worth the price? Without some major changes in the preposterous economic direction we have been lead, soon we will very likely find out.

Hitler scorned democracy as the haven of the weak, and he did blitz a number of them. Democracies can be weak and indecisive when standing before strong decisive leadership, but they need not be. They simply must be made more hospitable for the kind of good, strong, decisive leadership that the future will demand. No one who is afraid of change has ever led the way into the future. If democracy is not able to make the necessary changes to govern the emerging forces, there is another alternative that might be even more frightening that human tyranny, which is inhuman tyranny.

There are certain trends that stand out as we observe this evolution of power through history. First, the pace of change is radically increasing. The Military power base maintained its dominance for two to three thousand years. The Religious power base maintained its dominance for just a little more than one millennium. The Political power base dominated for just three or four centuries. This trend of acceleration is not only likely to continue, but increase. If so, how long can we expect the Economic power base to maintain its position? Is there another power base that will soon emerge? Or will one of the previously dominant power bases re-emerge as preeminent?

No sincere student of history can neglect the Bible as a source of insight, and interestingly, the scriptures both accurately predicted these trends in human affairs, and where we would go from here. Both Jesus and the apostles stated that this would happen "like birth pangs coming upon a woman." Many theologians, who obviously were not women, always predicted that this meant *quickly.* Actually birth pangs do not come upon a woman quickly, but they begin slowly and are relatively mild. As she gets closer to the birth, the contractions become both more intense and more frequent. This does closely parallel the pattern in which these forces have evolved through history.

It is also interesting that many theologians have seen the conclusion of these forces as being the end of the world, when Jesus and His followers pointed to it as the beginning of a new epoch in which peace, justice, and prosperity would prevail throughout the earth. This epoch begins when God intervenes in world affairs just in time to keep us from destroying ourselves. This intervention takes place during a time when there is a great "increase of knowledge." This certainly describes the period that we are now in, when more knowledge is now being added to the pool of human resources in three years than it took to accumulate over the last six thousand years of recorded history.

Regardless of whether you hold to the biblical view, if the trend of history is a foundation for perceiving the future, we are certainly entering a period where the forces are now so powerful that they seem far beyond the ability of humanity to control them. The rate of Economic change is now coming so fast that we are at the limits of our ability to react to those that have already happened, much less reach into the future to control them.

Computers are dramatically increasing in their speed and power, and are seemingly keeping just a breath ahead of the astonishing rate of change. We are quickly getting to the point where we will conceivably have to give the full authority and control to computers, and step out of their way, if they are going to keep up with the rate of change. Is this what we want to do? We should be thinking about this now because the decision will soon be upon us. We are entering a dimension where constant change is the *only* constant.

We must not be afraid of making the needed changes in our government, or our government will be doomed by the forces of change. This is not to imply that businessmen, or economists are going to be our saviors. Business, and especially American business, has its own act to clean up. The world is changing, and changing fast, and much of American business has abandoned its responsibility of leadership and has fallen to managing by reports of what happened last quarter—that's too late! True leadership is not managing where we have been, but where we are going. Neither is leadership just adjusting to the possibilities of the future—we must have the vision, resolve and character to make the future what it is to be.

THE NATURE OF FREEDOM

History has proven that humans are remarkably adaptable, but we do have limits. It is also apparent that we are fast approaching the point of overload with regard to change. As the historian Will Durant observed, "Without the grooves along which our minds can run with unconscious ease, we become perpetually hesitant, and gripped with insecurity." The end result of overwhelming insecurity is a mental shutdown, or insanity. If there were a way to analyze the composite mentality of civilization, we would certainly be judged somewhere between dysfunctional and insane, fast heading toward pushing back the outer envelope of raving mad.

Tradition provides the basic cultural grooves along which our minds are freed to run. Traditions provide for people the same kind of freedom that tracks provide for a train. We may at first think that tracks do not free a train, but rather restrict it, and this is true, but it is a restriction that frees. A train may be more "free" to roam across the land if the tracks were not there, but how far would it get? The tracks actually free the train to be what it was created to be. What good is it to have a great diesel engine with several thousand horsepower if we are stuck in the mud and just spinning our wheels?

If we were invited to a formal dinner with important dignitaries, but had never received any training in basic manners or protocol, we would most likely be insecure and have a difficult time functioning throughout the evening. However, if we had been trained, or just took a couple of hours to read an article on manners and protocol, we could go into the evening confident and "free," to both enjoy it and use the time properly. Likewise, even the greatest athlete would be rendered somewhere between hesitant and helpless in a game without knowledge of the basic rules.

Crime is not rising so dramatically just because kids are prone to do what is wrong, but mostly because they have not been taught what is right. This is the result of the massive assault on cultural traditions and morals. The technological change is coming so fast that it is hard enough to cope with by itself, but add to that the stripping away of traditions and moral values, and we are adding nitro to the glycerin—there will be an explosion! The result of this has even caused former California governor Jerry Brown, the quintessential political modernist and self-proclaimed "champion of change," to begin a retreat, proclaiming "I want to slow things down so I can understand them better."

Religious fundamentalism may have made the world sick, but the overreaction of society will not just make us sick—it will be fatal. Lawlessness is now increasing on an exponential curve. At a time when we most need sound traditional moorings, philosophical extremists are cutting them as fast as they can, and the fundamentalists have been the only ones trying to stop them. Many of these may be likewise promoting intolerable extremes, but we cannot allow this to push us off the other end into the abyss of moral and literal anarchy over which we are now tottering.

Presently, some in the media will try to caricature almost anyone who stands with resolve for moral or traditional values, but the day is very close when the world will be beating a path to their door seeking help. A sound, uncompromising moral constitution is quickly emerging as possibly the greatest asset of a true leader in any field. Such will alone be steady enough to read the compass into the future.

WE MUST NOT FORGET PEOPLE

I know only a handful of people who foresaw the imminent collapse of communism in Europe. None of these were Economic leaders, or Political leaders, they were Religious leaders. The religious leaders perceived this because they were not bogged down studying graphs and reports, they were involved with people. Regardless of the basic power of the epoch, there has never been a revolution until the common people decided to go along with it. Regardless of your place of leadership, if you do not keep your hand on the pulse of the common man, you will not be able to discern the forces and great changes that lie ahead.

One of the great, and possibly irresistible, forces now moving through people everywhere, is the determination to tear down the walls that separate people from one another. Most of the barriers erected between peoples are the devices of insecure leaders motivated by territorial preservation. If those in leadership do not recognize the fallacy in this and tear the walls down themselves, the people will rise up and do it. If the people have to do it, then the leaders will come down with their walls.

True leadership, like true religion, has a nobility of character that is repelled by the pseudo leadership of compulsion and fear. To stoop to such devises is to abdicate true authority, not confirm it. Of course laws and restraints are needed, especially now because of the release of lawlessness. But, as discussed concerning the nature of proper traditions, true law must possess a grace and dignity that frees people, instead of bind them with the oppression of fear.

True leadership will find the synthesis between people groups, without compelling them to be just like each other. The glory of the creation is its diversity—God obviously intended for it to be a symphony, not a solo. Every tree is different, every snowflake is different, even every person is different from every other person. The power of civilization to advance has been fueled by the ability of different people to learn how to work together.

The violence and destruction of civilization has always come when the differences were used as a point of conflict. Along with the powerful force moving throughout the world to tear down the walls that separate people from each other, there is a terrible force seeking to turn people against each other. Racism is possibly the most destructive human evil, and can be found as the basic motivation behind almost every war in history. I am not just speaking of physical bigotry, but spiritual bigotry as well. Racism is not just between physical races, but against people groups who are different from us, whether the differences are based on actual race, religion, culture, geography, or other factors that make people different.

We are now well into the age of the Economic power base. Business is, on its most basic level, simply human transactions. The greatest leaders during this epoch will be those who are the most successful in facilitating these transactions by building the bridges of interchange between people. The greatest enemies of progress in this age are those who erect barriers that cut off human transactions between peoples.

Chapter Four

The Vision And The Plan—The Two Pillars of Leadership

Effective leaders have accomplished their own goals; great leaders dictated the course of history, and though they may have passed from this earth long ago, their leadership still shapes the world. In this chapter we will address two essential qualities without which no one will be a successful leader.

HAVING A VISION, BEING GOAL ORIENTED

This is the fundamental qualification for leadership. By definition, you are not a leader unless someone will follow you. Only a fool will follow someone who does not know where he is going.

Not only must a leader have goals but the *goals must be specific.* The more clearly defined the goal, the more likely it is that others will follow. Having a goal that is too general may be worse than not having one at all. General goals are seldom attained and lead only to frustration. Those who "want to get rich," or "go into business for themselves," seldom do.

Our goals must be noble. Not only should we be specific in your direction, but we should be just as specific about *why* we are going there. It is the energy which comes from having a worthy purpose that inspires others to the sacrifice and discipline required to succeed. If our goals are selfish we will only inspire selfishness; then we are not leaders but opportunists. The more selfless and noble our goals, the more inspirational they will be.

However, nobility in goals cannot be faked; pretenders to this will be found out. Just as we "are what we eat" physically, we are what we partake of intellectually and spiritually. The same period of time that selfishness has been in vogue in the west directly reflects western decline. The goal oriented and selfless Japanese quickly filled the void. The emptiness and superficiality of self-centeredness is now becoming apparent to everyone. Seeking the higher purposes will result in personal inspiration as well as the inspiration of others.

Great leaders have the ability to make other leaders followers. The quality of those who follow you will directly reflect the quality of your accomplishment. To make other leaders followers requires a greater depth of character, commitment and vision. The more intelligent and noble your goals are, the more intelligent and noble your followers will be.

Martin Luther King, Jr. was a great leader. He shared his dream with such conviction that it became the dream of millions of others. I heard it said by one of his associates that during the meetings with other civil rights leaders he would sit patiently, intently listening to everything which was said. He *was genuinely concerned with what others believed* and considered it important to understand them. This in turn made them more inclined to listen to him. Because he was always so intently listening he would inevitably be asked to share his thoughts. His words would then come with such profound understanding, clarity of purpose and confidence in his direction, there was little left to be said when he finished. Great leaders are usually more inclined to listen than to speak. Therefore, when they do speak it is with greater substance.

Great leaders have seldom taken the mantle of leadership for its own sake. True leadership is born out of vision and strategy that is established firmly on the bedrock of conviction and purpose. Leadership is a means and not the end in itself. By keeping this in mind we can ennoble our specific, material goals. For example, few will be inspired if your goal is to be the biggest company in a certain field (specific goal), but many might become inspired if your goal for doing that is to better the economic conditions of your community, help send the children of your faithful, long-term employees to college, etc.

CULTIVATING VISION

The ability to be a great visionary is to a degree a spiritual gift that some are just born with. However, many who seem to naturally have this gift lack other characteristics such as resolve, steadfastness, etc., to make their visions a reality. These are dreamers who may talk a lot but seldom do much. There are many others who have all of the characteristics to take a vision and make it a reality, but have difficulty formulating the vision. However, this ability can be cultivated by those who desire it enough to apply themselves.

By definition, a vision is a concept that is not yet real. The first step in formulating a vision is to simply start thinking about what could be rather than what presently exists. This does take a certain amount of optimism; the critical and skeptical will seldom have visions or dreams.

To be optimistic is no small feat—recent studies revealed that almost 70% of the average American's thoughts were negative (thinking something bad about someone or something, or expecting something bad to happen). The shocking fact of this study was that these were Americans who tend to be the most optimistic people in the world! Why do we allow ourselves to live in such mental misery? Such people live lives that are mostly bitter, and fall well below their potential. Only those who believe that they can succeed will be encouraged enough to put forth the effort that it takes to succeed.

The single most important step that most of us can take to start becoming visionary, and then turning our visions into successes, is to start thinking the very best about everything and everyone. Even if we are sometimes wrong by doing this, it is much better to err on the side of believing in others than in doubting them, not to mention the fact that our lives will become infinitely more enjoyable!

Every event that takes place in our lives will either make us bitter or better, but the choice ours. Every failure can make us wiser and stronger. Thomas Edison tried over a thousand experiments that failed before he tried the one that resulted in the light bulb. Those one thousand experiments were not wasted; each one taught him a little more about what electricity was and what it was not. Soon he had the proper equation so surrounded that it simply could not escape him. It was extraordinary vision, grounded upon a resolve that he simply would not give up, which made Edison a great inventor. Such resolve is impossible without optimism, which is the basic belief that you will ultimately succeed.

Start practicing vision right where you are. Look at your job and list all of the positive things about it. Then begin a list of things that could make it better. Then determine that you are going to accomplish these and make it the very best job that it can be. As Martin Luther King, Jr. once said, "If you're a street sweeper, determine that you are going to be the very best street sweeper that ever lived. If you become the best at what you do, even if it is sweeping streets, the whole world will beat a path to your door and declare: 'Here lives the best street sweeper that ever lived.'"

Start practicing this in every area of your life. If your marriage is not going well, determine that you are going to make it better. If you would bring your wife flowers occasionally she might start to want to lose weight; she might stop complaining about the petty things you do to bother her. You may have to humble yourself to do this, but the one who can humble himself will always be the one of greatest character and strength.

The measure of who you were in this life will be remembered mostly by those things that you were able to make better than they were. Practice this in every area of your life. Count your successes and measure your progress. You'll find that each success will lead to other bigger ones. If you learn what it takes to turn your marriage around you may be able to then turn a company around, or a city. Build your life on successes, advancement, and you will grow in the ability to improve the conditions of everything and everyone in your life. From this it becomes natural to see that everything and everyone can be better, which is the essence of vision.

EXERCISE:

For a simple but effective exercise in developing vision, specify your goals. Take a few minutes to write them down. To help you might want to answer the following questions, then add to them your own.

General Life Goal: What is the most important goal that you want to accomplish in your life? (Possible answers might be to write a book, build a business, get elected to a public office, become a church leader, etc.)

Family Goal: What is the most important goal for your family? (Consider each member separately. You might ask them their goals and make yours seeing them all accomplished.)

Financial Goal: What is your personal financial goal? (Here it might be anything from owning your home and being out of debt by a certain age, to having a certain net worth, or becoming financially independent.)

Pleasure Goal: What is your greatest goal for recreation or pleasure? (This could include such things as owning a vacation home, a boat, becoming a private pilot, etc.)

It could be helpful for you to write each goal in a journal so that you can review each one periodically to measure your progress. This leads us to the next foundational characteristic of true leaders:

THE ABILITY TO FORMULATE A PLAN

This is the main characteristic which separates the *achievers* from the dreamers. An ancient proverb declares, "He who fails to plan, plans to fail." Even if we have the most noble and appropriate goals, our chances of accomplishing them are remote without proper planning.

More than genius, it was probably Napoleon's commitment to planning that made him so much more successful than the rival generals he defeated. He studied incessantly, pouring over the maps of potential battlefields, intelligence reports of the disposition and strength of the enemy, even the character and history of opposing generals.

Like most enterprises, battles are seldom executed as planned, but Napoleon was such a tireless planner he would have fought the battle many times in his mind before the real one took place. This helped prepare him for meeting each contingency. He would have his revised plan being implemented while his adversaries were just getting out their maps to start thinking about what they should do next. By this he was almost always able to stay one step ahead of his opponents, keeping them on the defensive and providing opportunities which were not available to those less prepared. Planning can do the same for us.

Planning is both an art and a discipline. Even the greatest artist must develop his skills; so must the leader develop his ability to plan. Effective planning requires the ability to assimilate and organize facts concerning the realities being dealt with. Then we must be able to observe the facts in a way that will produce insights that will lead to advantage and success. Let's briefly break down this process into its three basic parts:

1. State the goal(s). This was done in our previous exercise. Planning requires an ability to visualize the future and then to make a road map for navigating it. We will never know where to make the road if we do not know where we want to go.

2. Getting and organizing the necessary facts. The ability to do research is a significant skill within itself. We must determine first where we can get the best and most relevant facts to help us. How do we sift through all of the information available to us to get just what we need? This is where many leaders get bogged down, because they are concept oriented instead of detail oriented. This is the point where their leadership potential is often lost.

3. Making the plan. A first step in making a good plan is the realization that the plan can be changed. Do not worry about having to make a perfect plan because you will be able to make adjustments as you go. As a pilot I always had to file a flight plan before departure, but many times changing or unforecast weather or other conditions forced changes in the plan. I soon recognized that it was just as important for me to know when and how to adjust my plan as it was to make one—the plan just got me off the ground and going in the right direction. That will be the nature of many of our plans, but without them we would not even get started.

The best place to start making a plan is to state the goals or objectives. Then state the first step and succeeding ones to the conclusion. Important factors to include in the plan may be priorities, actions required, timing, personnel, other required resources, ways to measure progress toward the goal, etc.

> **EXERCISE:**
> Take the goals that you listed before and write out a plan for each one. Write questions that come to your mind such as: What is the first step I need to take? What will the subsequent steps be? What may present obstacles to accomplishing the goal? What can present opportunities for accomplishing it? What resources will I need? What resources are available? Who has accomplished this goal before and how did they do it? It might be good to lay out one year, five year plans, etc.

If you were the enemy of your plan, what steps would you take to stop it from succeeding? This will help you to see potential weakness or serious problems which are not readily apparent from your own perspective.

Chapter Five

Character, Will And Wisdom

History testifies that even the most outstanding leaders will still ultimately fail, regardless of their brilliance, unless their lives have the underpinnings of honor, morality and character. In this part we will examine some of the more profound characteristics that constitute this essential foundation for success in leadership. The first is:

THE WILL TO IMPLEMENT THE PLAN

In the last chapter we covered the essential need for leaders to have vision and the ability to plan. Many have had these abilities and yet still failed because they did not have the resolve, courage and endurance to implement their plans.

"Knowledge is power" according to a biblical proverb. Knowledge is essential for accomplishing every endeavor, and we will do well to seek knowledge. However, without adding to our knowledge wisdom and courage, we will probably accomplish very little, regardless of how much knowledge we have. *Wisdom is the **Ability** to apply knowledge correctly. Courage is the **Will** to apply it.* Without wisdom and courage, increased knowledge will only inflict us with "the paralysis of analysis." Planning and preparation must lead to action, which is the implementation of our plans.

It is quite unlikely that one will ever feel, or be, totally prepared and confident when the action begins. If we wait for complete confidence in any endeavor it is likely that we will never start anything, much less accomplish anything. Often circumstances come upon us suddenly which require action when we feel totally unprepared. In these situations it seems that once we begin to take action, confidence and wisdom then come. A leader must be action oriented and not just a whiz at theory and planning. The ability to plan is essential for true success, but it must be united with action.

A leader, like the captain of a ship, needs to know where he's going and how to get there *before* he leaves port. He must also be able to make adjustments in his plans during the journey, after the storms, mechanical failures and other surprises make them necessary. It is important to have the resolution to stay on the course when possible, but it is just as important to know when to adjust the course, or to get back to the course when a deviation has been required. Had that wisdom been with Captain Smith of the Titanic, it is likely that his ship would never have sunk. Resolve to hold the course is important, but it can be deadly when it is not balanced with wisdom.

KEEPING PRIORITIES

Many have their leadership abilities sapped by majoring on minors. A popular saying in business today is "count the pennies and the dollars will take care of themselves." This is probably true because if we are the leader of our organization and we are taking our time to count the pennies we probably will not have any dollars to worry about! Get someone else to count the pennies! The leader must major on the majors.

If we do not take control of our own time, that which represents 10% or less of our enterprise will demand 90% of our attention. In many cases this is the cause of burnout for the leader and substantial losses for the enterprise. If we're in leadership we must learn to delegate the details and give our attention to leading and planning. This is hard for leaders because by nature they are doers and are inclined to become involved—but it must be done if we are to fulfill our potential.

Learning to prioritize your duties can actually multiply your productivity. A simple classification system can be helpful. Keep a current list of your "Things To Do." If under your classification system 1 is the highest priority, do not work on the 2's until the 1's are finished, and so forth down the line. A few more pennies may fall through the cracks, but you'll be amazed at how many more dollars come in!

If we are going to be able to keep our priorities in their proper order, we must be delivered from the curse of self-centeredness. Few empires, civilizations, or enterprises have been overthrown by enemies without—they have almost all perished from the cancer of self-centeredness, which is often the result of their prosperity. Cancer is a cell that consumes for its own purposes without regard to the rest of the body. In a sense, cancer is the personification of self-centeredness.

In many areas Western civilization has risen to the highest standards of honor, justice, morality and the esteem for life. It is apparent that these qualities are the foundation of western progress. Now those foundations are being tested. It is not surprising that the issue of abortion is now becoming an issue almost as divisive as slavery was in the last century, and it has the potential to surpass it. However, the issue is not just abortion, it is the value we will give to life.

In nature the preservation of life is the most basic and powerful motivation. Because of this, excepting only a few of the most base forms of species, *family* is a primary drive of life. There are few creatures in existence that will not quickly and instinctively sacrifice their own lives to protect their young. It was no accident that the very first test of

Solomon's wisdom was over the issue of a mother's sanctity for life. The very first test of wisdom for any government is its commitment to the sanctity of life. Any parents who would sacrifice their young are not only subhuman, but would have difficulty finding acceptance even in the animal kingdom.

There will be no peace of mind or peace on earth until life is esteemed above selfish ambition or convenience. It is not only unnatural for a mother to destroy her child, born or unborn, but it reveals a fundamental departure from civilization to embrace a barbarism in its most base and inhuman form. The resolution of the abortion issue gives us the opportunity to provide the world leadership in finding even higher standards of morality, justice and the esteem for life. The failure to resolve it with courage and honor, not just with law, will certainly leave a major crack in our foundation of honor and morality, ultimately leading to tyranny.

Just because something is legal does not make it right. There are fundamental laws that prevail in nature which reveal a great deal more wisdom than politicians have been able to display. True morality does not have much to do with mere legal compliance; true morality is doing what is *right.* A civilization that is not based on law will be open to despotism and tyranny. But a civilization that cannot rise above the law to live by what is not just legal, but what is also moral, has lost its humanity and its potential for true greatness. Lawlessness always results in tyranny. The inability to rise above law will also result in tyranny. The preservation of life is fundamental to both nature and morality.

Even so, can we cast stones at the mother who aborts her child if we ourselves are sacrificing our living children at the altars of the petty gods of selfish ambition and personal success? Could even the greatest success of our enterprises be interpreted as anything but a terrible human failure if we lose our own children in the process? Who can count the "successful" businessmen, sportsmen, coaches and even church leaders who have accomplished their goals only to say that they would trade everything just to have their families back. The first condition that God said was not good was for man to be alone; it is not good, but we will end up there if we do not give our families the priority they deserve.

This book is not intended to be a family counseling manual. However, if you have a family, it will almost certainly either be a great source of motivation, or a great burden which detracts from your venture. What your family becomes to you will almost certainly be up to you. If you love your family more than you love your enterprise, you will probably love your enterprise, and everything else, more than you would if you loved it more than your family. As stated, the decline in American productivity parallels the devotion to selfishness, which is the primary factor in the decline of the American family. Family is primordial. History testifies that the quickest way to destroy a civilization is to destroy the moral fabric which is rooted in the esteem for family. All other standards of meaning and morality are easily overthrown if the basic drive of life—the family—is diluted.

After our immediate family the next on our priority list should be people. Do we see our venture as a "thing" or as the people who comprise it. People are more important than things, and as you personalize your venture, some of the more powerful motivations for success will energize your people. A primary goal of the leader should be to get his people to, as much as possible, see themselves as a family. Such an identity will be your best chance to stir them to self-sacrifice in place of the self-centeredness that always works against the basic vision and purpose of your venture.

STEADFASTNESS

Steadfastness was originally a navy term for the ability to stay on course. We could add to this that it is also the ability to keep returning to the course after a deviation is necessary, until the goal is accomplished. To achieve this, the goal will have to have more power in your life than the multitude of external pressures which will try to deter you from the course. The ability to do this will depend mostly upon how well you have prepared for the journey to accomplishment, with its conflicts and its storms.

As an aircraft pilot, several times I have been caught in storms so rough I could not read my charts. I would have been in serious trouble had I not taken the time to *prepare* for the flight. During those storms I was thankful I had not taken any shortcuts in my training, and that I was conscientious enough to study my flight path before I took off.

In preparation for every flight I would memorize the important frequencies and headings, along with an alternate airport with good weather that I could reach with my available fuel. I regularly reviewed emergency procedures for possible engine failure, which instruments I would lose if my vacuum, electrical or other systems failed, and how I could compensate for their loss, etc. On the majority of my flights this may have all seemed like a waste of time, but there were a few occasions when I knew that all of my effort in planning and training had been worth it. I have had several engine failures, experienced lightning strikes, electrical fires, and have been blown far off course by storms. In most of these incidents my pulse hardly even quickened because I was *prepared* and knew what to do. A lack of preparedness can result in panic which is potentially more deadly than the emergency. Every enterprise will have emergencies. Our preparation during times of relative calm will have much to do with our performance during the crisis.

Peace of mind is one of the most valuable assets of a leader. Worry clouds our judgment and saps more energy than much physical exertion; stress is the worst enemy of clear thinking and planning. Besides preparation for the course, there are other factors which will help us to keep our peace of mind.

General Robert E. Lee and Stonewall Jackson were pious men who had a genuine belief that there was One higher than they who ordered the affairs of men. This enabled them to maintain a peace of mind even during the times of greatest conflict, confusion and pressure. This was such a great advantage that some historians have suggested that it was the greatest advantage that these great generals had over their opponents. Peace of mind is certainly one of the greatest human possessions and advantages that we can have in life, and it should be a goal itself. Worry will never cause what we want to happen, or keep what we do not want from happening—it is a trivial, useless exercise that is unworthy of the true leader.

ENDURANCE

This is the ability to stay with the task all the way to *completion*, which is similar to steadfastness. This is a serious problem with those who have strong leadership ability because leaders find it much more stimulating to start a task than to finish it. As a result they often have numerous unfinished projects lying dormant while they pick up the pursuit of the next interesting venture.

The ability to finish the job is every bit as important as being able to get all of the resources and energy going to start it. This takes **discipline**. The failure to complete jobs is usually a telltale sign that we are running on emotional energy rather than true, focussed vision. This is the reason some of the world's best salesmen remain poor; they can get an eskimo excited about buying snow, but somehow they never get his signature on the bottom line. These salesmen get a sense of accomplishment out of persuading their prospects to believe them—not in getting their business. We have not succeeded *until* the job is completed!

INTEGRITY

Integrity is more than just being honest, it is doing what is *right*. It is the freedom from corrupting influence or practice. It is practicing what you preach. It is doing what your conscience tells you to do even if it leaves you as a committee of one. It is the courage to stand by your convictions. It is always reaching for higher moral standards than may be customary in "the group," for the true leader is always reaching for higher standards. It is also the courage and honesty to admit mistakes and failures, and to accept the blame for them.

Even the greatest leaders make mistakes. The better the leader you are the more costly and visible your mistakes will be. Recovering from mistakes is an important test of true leadership ability. Complete recovery will not take place without accepting such mistakes and taking responsibility for them. The greatest leaders learn to turn their failures into opportunities for achievement and victory. In many cases failures will turn into the best opportunities for victory. Wellington, Napoleon and Lee accomplished some of their greatest victories because of their ability to turn their enemy's achievements into a trap for defeating them. The Japanese used defeat in war as a springboard for economic victory in peacetime. Vision and leadership can turn the worst catastrophe into opportunity.

To his credit General Lee never blamed anyone but himself for the defeat at Gettysburg. His subordinates failed him a number of times in that battle; the compounded effect of these failures led him to make the desperate decision that led to defeat. But Lee never mentioned any of his subordinate's failures. After the war when one of these generals publicly and bitterly blamed Lee for the defeat, Lee agreed with him. This humility endeared him to the entire world; he actually became the most respected man in the nation after the war— even among the Northerners. His humility soon caused even his worst critics to acknowledge him as one of the great men of their times.

Historians have declared that Lee's leadership after his defeat was probably greater than that which he displayed in war. Almost all agree that his leadership in helping to bring reconciliation between the North and South was more important for the restoration of the nation than any other single factor. Lee set a standard of personal integrity, reconciliation and forgiveness. His leadership after the war almost certainly prevented years of guerilla warfare and further destruction in a nation that desperately needed healing.

A great leader must possess the confidence and security to accept the truth about himself and the consequences of his actions. The greatest leaders are those who can best deal with failure—because all will fail at one time or another. Those who boast that they have never failed have never really played the game. But failure truly can be a great opportunity for future success, if we learn the lessons it teaches instead of just making excuses. As the saying goes, "He who is good at making excuses is seldom good at anything else." The greatest victories are those which overcome previous defeats.

Those who follow you or work for you deserve to know the facts. People usually see far more than the average leader gives them credit for. When we are not straightforward about problems and mistakes it will ultimately result in a deterioration of morale and commitment as they will think that we are either not honest, or unable to see reality. Motivation and loyalty that has depth and staying power is founded upon truth, not hype.

Honesty is also an essential requirement for peace of mind. We'll never have peace if we're worried about someone finding us out. Whatever we may gain by cheating or lying is not worth the price we pay when we are forty years old with an eighty year-old heart. Honesty brings respect and inspires those who may serve under us more than almost anything else we can do. The self-respect we gain from being honest will pay higher dividends in the long run than anything we might gain through deception.

COURAGE

Courage is the quality of mind and heart that makes us resist the temptation to stop or retreat in the face of opposition, danger, or hardship. This implies the summoning of all of our powers to reach the goal. Courage is the firmness of spirit and moral backbone which, while appreciating and properly measuring the risks involved, makes us press on until success is accomplished.

Before almost any worthy goal is attained there will be obstacles and roadblocks. How we deal with these problems will determine our success or failure. There are four basic ways that people deal with problems; two of these ways lead to certain failure, one of them will make success more difficult. Only one of these ways of dealing with problems is *likely* to lead to success. Let us consider them each separately.

The first way we can respond to an obstacle is to let it turn us back. This course leads to failure and reveals the lack of courage, resolve and leadership required for success in any enterprise.

The second way is to let the obstacle stop us. We may not retreat or turn back, but we no longer advance either. Even if we hold on to our dream or goal, if we allow obstacles to stop us, we will be perpetually defeated and frustrated.

The third way to deal with an obstacle is to let it change our course. There are some obstacles we meet which require a change in our plans that would make this option the best one. Just changing our course may still allow us to go on to ultimate success, *but if we are prone to letting obstacles change our course too easily the chances of our success will greatly decrease.*

It takes wisdom to know when to change our plan. Sometimes we must let wisdom overrule courage and resolve if we are going to succeed. It may have required more courage and resolve for Hitler to insist on taking Leningrad, but it was also unwise and it led to his ultimate defeat, not just at Leningrad but for the entire war. To conquer Leningrad was one of Hitler's goals, but it was not essential for accomplishing his overall goal of conquering Russia. If he had just gone around that city he probably could have accomplished his ultimate goal. His insistence on taking that one fortress resulted in the wasting of an entire army, needlessly destroyed in that one battle. Resolve and courage are essential, but they must be controlled by intelligence.

The fourth way to deal with an obstacle is to *overcome* it, driving it out of your way instead of allowing it to drive you off of your course. This is usually the best way to deal with an obstacle and should be our first approach.

Courage is essential to leadership but it must be tempered with vision and strategy, always keeping our ultimate goal in the forefront so that we are not defeated by our secondary successes. George Washington is a study in how to balance courage with keeping our vision on the ultimate goal. Many times ambitious men rose up to seek his position as Commander-in-Chief of the Continental Army. Often he was tempted to defend himself and attack the integrity of those lesser men. He resisted that temptation knowing that such pettiness could undo the unity of the thirteen states, which would result in their defeat by the British. It took more courage for Washington to stay above the political infighting than it did to get elected.

LOYALTY

Loyalty is faithfulness to principles, to the plan and to people. A social chameleon who changes to conform to each new environment or group is void of the basic characteristics that makes a true leader. True leaders are not so easily changed but instead have the strength of character to change their environments, or the mindset of the crowd.

If we are to expect others to be loyal to us we must set the example. If we possess loyalty we will not stoop to gossip or to belittle others in leadership, or those who may be subordinate. The true leader does not rise by making others look smaller. Great leaders set their standards by the highest standards, not by what others may or may not be doing.

INITIATIVE

Obviously a leader has to be one who seeks and accepts responsibility. Half of the victory is often found in just starting the battle. The ones who take initiative will usually be able to keep it, giving them a substantial advantage.

It has been said that there are basically three kinds of people in the world: those who watch what is happening, those who talk about making things happen, *and those who actually do it.* The sad thing is that most of those in the first two categories have everything required to be a "doer" except one thing—initiative. Many of the greatest athletes never play in a real game because they never took the first step to try out for the team. If those who spend their lives dreaming about being great musicians would spend as much time practicing as they do dreaming, others would be dreaming about being them! Few of those who are always talking about doing great things ever do anything at all, much less anything great. Every journey begins with just one step; if you do not know how to take it you are not going to go anywhere.

Chapter Six

Motivating People

The quality of a leader's accomplishments will depend upon the quality of the people who are willing to follow him, and the degree of sacrifice and commitment they are willing to make. People must have a reason for the commitment to make sacrifices. The leaders ability to attract the best people, and to keep them motivated will depend on his understanding of what motivates his people, and of what hinders their motivation.

There are two basic kinds of motivation: positive and negative. Both work, and both can work well, depending on the circumstance and the people. Just about everyone will work hard if he fears that his job, his farm, or his business are in jeopardy. That is negative motivation. However, in some circumstances, such as jobs requiring creativity, few can produce their best work under this kind of pressure. They usually require a positive form of motivation. The effective leader has to be able to determine which type of motivation is appropriate and when to use it.

The Southern troops who served under General Lee held a significant advantage in motivation over their Northern counterparts throughout the war. Because of this they continually won battles against overwhelming odds. They had negative motivation in trying to preserve their way of life, but they had positive motivation in their love and trust for their leader. Few generals have been able to inspire the kind of devotion Lee inspired. After the war even his enemies called him one of the greatest leaders ever produced by this nation, and when he died the entire nation mourned his loss. What was his secret?

THE TWO KINDS OF LEADERS

There are basically two kinds of leaders: those who sacrifice the people for themselves, and those who sacrifice themselves for the people. Lee was one of the most striking examples of the latter. From the day he took command until Appomattox, he refused to sleep in anything but a tent, even when he visited Richmond, because he so identified himself with the hardship that his men were enduring. Twice when he tried to lead his men in a charge, the troops refused to let him, crying over and over, "General Lee to the rear!" To his men he was not some distant personage they only occasionally glimpsed getting out of his limo; he was one of them. They did not follow him just because of the stars on his shoulder, but because of his extraordinary character as a leader.

Napoleon also captured the devotion of his troops by identifying with the common man. Calling himself "the little corporal," he considered the time spent meeting personally with his troops an important part of his battle plans. Few have continued to be effective leaders after they lost touch with the men in the trenches, on the assembly line, or in the pew. Any leader that loses touch with, or ceases to care for, his people, can probably be replaced by a good computer.

It is often taught in business and military leadership courses that leaders must distance themselves from their troops because "familiarity breeds contempt." There are some other good reasons for this, such as the fact that it becomes difficult to give orders to close friends, but the primary reason is because it is assumed that if a leader becomes too well known by his troops they will lose their respect for him. This is true for the typical leader whose authority is established more by his position than by his character, but a true leader will be even more respected the better he is known by his followers. True authority will pass the test of this kind of close examination. Those who attained the highest standards of true leadership were almost always comfortable with, and usually enjoyed, the company of even the lowest ranks of their followers. This usually inspired a level of sacrifice on the part of their followers that was a foundation of their significant accomplishments.

UNDERSTANDING THE SOUL OF YOUR VENTURE

One critical factor which must be understood in relation to motivation is that every entity, whether it is an enterprise or a nation, has a "soul" of its own, a unique identity. This soul is a composite of people, history and vision. The true nature and strength of this soul will become most apparent during a crisis, because when it is threatened the facades are stripped away so that its true nature is revealed. In this way, even a minor crisis can help the leader to understand the true nature of his enterprise so that he will be able to lead it even more effectively in a major crisis, or in times of no crisis.

Without understanding the soul of his enterprise, the leader is not only in a weakened position, he is in the wrong position. Those who take on the soul of the enterprise are followers; the leader should be the one who gives definition to the soul of the enterprise. The success of every venture is dependent on the performance of its people. Having those in your enterprise identify with the soul and territory of the enterprise is a fundamental key to your success and longevity. To help your people become bonded to the soul of your enterprise must be a high priority for the successful leader. To do this he must clearly define its purpose in a manner with which the people can understand and identify.

Britain's soul was tested by Napoleon and prevailed. Over a century later it was tested again by Hitler and prevailed. The same two tried the soul of Russia to their own destruction. The conflict in Afghanistan was not a true test of the Russian soul, no more than Vietnam was of the American, *because men are territorial; the soil is where you will usually find the identity of his soul.* Remove a man from his own land and his resolve will usually slip away, because his identity becomes blurred. Britain would give away all of her colonies with hardly a fight, but woe to the one who touches the British Isles! On its own soil, the Confederate Army in the Civil War was nearly invincible until it simply ran out of men. In Southern territory the Army of the Potomac (the Union) just did not have the resolve it displayed when its own land was threatened.

The soul of an army will obviously be tied to the nation it represents, but it can also be linked to ideals such as freedom, democracy, etc. If the soul of an army is tied to such ideals it should be understood that its morale will disintegrate in any conflict that is not directly related to its soul. For example, it proved impossible for the United States to keep the morale of its army high in Vietnam because its soul is strongly linked to the preservation of liberty, and it could not remain motivated when asked to help defend the government of a dictator. If you are going to take your venture beyond the realm of its soul identity, you must make some basic adjustments, and often accept the fact that its performance will suffer.

The soul of a business is directly tied to its product. Productivity will be closely linked to the leader's ability to have his people identified with their product. One good way to do this is to link the identity of the product with a city, region, or a larger organization. The automobile industry successfully did this with Detroit; Boeing aircraft did it with Seattle, etc. The people who work for those industries know that their products represent their city, which is their families and friends.

A sports team's soul will be linked to the game it plays. Championships, recognition and rewards will certainly help to motivate the players, but all of these must be built upon the primary motivation of a love for the game. If a player loses his love for the game, other motivations may allow him to do well, but his full potential will never be realized. A coach's first priority should always be to instill and maintain in the players a love for the game.

A coach's second priority should be to link his team to the city, region, or organization for which they play. A wise college coach will impart to his team a strong sense that they are out their fighting for their school, which represents the state, the alumni, etc. Wise professional team owners try to get their players rooted in their community because they realize the added motivation that this carries. Constant trading of players will erode this and reduce their loyalty to working for the highest bidder, which the fans recognize, affecting their loyalty to the teams. This is why some of the winning teams of late cannot even fill their home stadiums, especially if there are any other recreational interests in the area.

A church, that is a true church and not just a business, has her identity in the Lord that it worships. It is obvious that the true Product of many Christian churches is not Christ, but rather a particular doctrine, the personality of the pastor, or even certain projects or goals it seeks to attain. These have a "soul" that is more like a typical corporation than the biblical faith, and their leaders often have more in common with executives than prophets. Many of these leaders are becoming somewhat more honest about this, openly declaring their unbelief, but if their true Product, or purpose is not Christ, would it not be even more honest to drop His name altogether? Using a Christian church to perpetrate philosophies contrary to Christ's own teachings is so obviously dishonest that it is easy to understand why there is such confusion, disloyalty and hypocrisy in the church at large. True motivation and long-term success will always be directly linked to honesty.

This is not to negate the fact that there are honest church leaders and true believers, and it is understandable why these churches are now growing at an unprecedented rate, while the others are likewise shrinking.

Loyalty will only be as strong as the "soul links" in any organization. There are other things that can motivate to a degree, such as bonuses, personal recognition, etc., but these should never be seen as the primary motivation. It does not matter how much charisma we may possess, as leaders, we cannot really impart to others substance that we ourselves do not have. The effective leader cannot lose touch with his basic purpose, or Product. A soldier must love his country if he is expected to risk his life for it and motivate his men to do the same. If he has lost his passion for the game, the success of a coach will be limited at best. If you have lost your own love and faith in the gospel your converts will be few. The effective leader must guard against majoring on minors. Know the heart or "soul" of your enterprise and lay hold of it with a grip that only death can loosen.

THE SOURCE OF AUTHORITY

Our authority might be defined as the degree of our leadership and the limits of its jurisdiction. For example, a corporate president may have considerable respect from his workers with matters related to their business, but have little authority to influence their political views.

There are two basic aspects to authority. The first aspect we will call "legal." This is authority that is tangible because it is a position held, such as foreman, captain, president, judge, etc. The second aspect of authority we will call "spiritual." Spiritual authority is more intangible because it is a respect that must be earned. A shop foreman may be given the legal authority to lead his shop, and people will obey his orders because of his position. However, if this foreman is not well liked or respected he will have little spiritual authority over his people, therefore they will probably not do their best job for him.

Once a legal position of authority is attained, it should be the endeavor of the leader to then build a solid foundation of spiritual authority if he is to get the best results. In many cases spiritual authority can have greater influence over the people being led than the legal authority will have. Anyone who has been in the military learns quickly that a sergeant, who may not possess the legal authority of a lieutenant, or captain, may actually have more influence over the men in the heat of battle than the officers will. Therefore, the wise officer learns to work through the sergeants, concentrating on the development of their own authority, or influence, with them.

Legal authority comes strictly from the position, but the basis for spiritual authority comes from experience, integrity of character, and the love for the product or purpose for the venture. It is usually experience that gives the sergeant more real authority or influence than less experienced officers who hold a higher rank. A high degree of spiritual authority can be attained simply by the respect that others have for a consistently honest and noble character.

A good example of how a love for the product can translate into spiritual authority is the experience a friend of mine had in school. A teacher's product is the ability to impart useful knowledge to their students. My friend was having such difficulty with math that it appeared to both him and his teachers that he was just destined to be hopelessly inept in that subject. However, in the seventh grade he found himself in the class of a different kind of math teacher. She had such a genuine love for mathematics that she was contagious with it. She did not just teach the subject, she imparted such a love for the subject that her students would teach themselves. My friend not only excelled in math that year, but for the rest of his time in school, and remains so enthralled with it that now, many years later, in his spare time he still enjoys the challenge of difficult mathematical problems. A teacher that was a true leader took what had been a dread and turned it into a passion; she did it by simply having that passion herself.

A foreman who has a true love for his craft, and can impart it to his workers, will always have the best shop. A coach who loves his game more, and can impart that love, will usually have the best team. A sailor who can impart a love for ships and sea will have the best crew. Those with the most love for their product will be the best leaders because they will spend more of their own time and energy learning about it.

When I was doing some part-time flight instructing I met an Air Force pilot who helped me to substantially improve my own skills, simply because of his passion for airplanes. He was a transport pilot and flew an average of about 120 hours per month. He then used all of the money he made (he was not married) to go around to civilian airports renting planes to fly around in. When he ran out of money he would often ask to ride with me as I was teaching just so he could be in the air. Whenever a unique airplane landed at our airport he would be the first one out to investigate it, asking the owner dozens of questions, and usually getting permission to take it up for a quick flight. I watched as his love for planes infected the other pilots and instructors with a new zeal for precision and knowledge of our craft. He unquestionably led all of us to a new level of excellence in our profession, and he was not the least bit aware of it. Whenever I think of the great pilots I have known, he is always one of the first to come to mind. Whenever I think of the great leaders I have known, which includes Air Force generals and Navy admirals who were crack fighter pilots, this young lieutenant is right up there with them.

A true passion that burns in the heart of a leader will be contagious. A biblical proverb states that "a chord of three strands cannot be easily broken." In the case of leadership authority the three strands are: position, integrity and love for the product. The position is legal, but integrity and love are spiritual forces that carry much more power than that of a mere legal position.

A true teacher does not just impart truths, but a love for the truth. This is a power that cannot be faked. If you do not have passion for what you do, you do not have leadership, regardless of how well you may know the principles and formulas. True leadership is a powerful spiritual force that can only come from your heart; true leadership is an impartation of your own soul to others. Understanding this "soul," that is both individual and also found in the unity of those gathered for a common purpose, is fundamental to understanding leadership, and to having it.

There are politicians who are pretenders to the throne of true leadership and authority in every type of enterprise. A pure politician cannot and will not be a true leader. A true leader may be in politics but he will not be a politician. A true leader that holds a political position would be more accurately termed a statesman. By definition a politician is motivated by political expediency, a force which erodes true conviction and conscience which is the very foundation of true leadership. To the politician the position is the goal. A statesman will care little for position or title; he will be devoted to results and will see the position as merely a means to accomplishing his purpose.

In government, especially within a democracy, politicians have their useful place. In the legislative branch they may accurately reflect the will of the people to which they are so sensitive. The legislative branches of the federal and state governments are comprised almost entirely of followers, not leaders. Very few legislators are original, innovative thinkers; they usually try to just flow with the stream. There are exceptions to this but they are rare. The nations best leaders will almost always be found in the arenas of business, sports, the military, or missions.

True leaders are repulsed by politics and bored by legislative procedure. The executive and judicial branches of government were designed to be led by appointees for this reason. It is taken for granted that the president will be a leader type and therefore would appoint leaders to the cabinet and judicial positions. When a mere politician wins the presidency he will often be threatened by true leaders and therefore will seldom appoint them to high positions. When the executive and judicial branches of government are not led by true leaders we are destined to pay a high price through inefficiency, ineffectiveness, or worse. To be effective these branches of government must be led by those who are moved more by the power of their convictions than the clamor of the people.

OWNERSHIP AND MOTIVATION

The failure of socialism is rooted in the lack of ownership. The first colonies in America were communes. Even though their lives depended on productivity in the common gardens, many starved because of a lack of it. This was the result of general laziness and lack of devotion from the people who ended up being the very ones who starved! When the people were given their own plots of land and told to grow their own food, productivity *multiplied.*

When a nation begins to target the wealthy for taxes they are actually penalizing success and promoting mediocrity and the lack of initiative. This practice inevitably dilutes the fuel of the economic engine of that nation. Again, the soul of man is profoundly linked to ownership; productivity is profoundly linked to reward. Man's motivation, energy and concentration are directly tied to these two basic principles.

The history of the U.S. social services also testifies to the power of ownership, even when it comes to charities. Bureaucratic benevolence has proven itself to be a definition of inefficiency; only a fraction of the capital devoted to social services actually reaches a person in need. One who has been rewarded for his initiative and success will be far more effective in everything he does, including helping the poor. Not all charities are efficient but those operated or overseen by successful entrepreneurs tend to be many times more efficient than comparable government agencies. This is because the volunteer entrepreneurs start thinking of these charities as *their* charities and they become utterly committed to their success. The point is not how much money is being spent on the needy but how many of their needs are actually being met. As Winston Churchill once said, "Socialism will only work in two places: in heaven, where they don't need it, and in hell, where they already have it!"

It is true that wealth gained by inheritance, or power and influence gained through aristocracy, have not historically been considerate of the less fortunate. But the voluntary charity of successful, self-made entrepreneurs is surprisingly generous. If we stopped taxing to support the inefficient social services on the condition that the taxpayer gave that amount to a charity, there probably would not be a homeless or hungry person in the land. Again, even charity is bound up in ownership. There are great emotional and spiritual rewards that come from giving to the less fortunate. There is no such reward when you are forced to give through taxation. The government usurps this opportunity by implementing an impersonal bureaucracy. As Churchill also stated, "If at age twenty one is not a liberal he has no heart. If at age forty he is not a conservative he has no *mind!*"

A fundamental commission of true leadership is to give ownership to the people. Their job must be *their* job. The company needs to be *their* company. The mission needs to be *their* mission, etc. The more people identify the enterprise as theirs the more productive and successful it will become. This does not necessarily mean stock options for employees (even though they have been effective); it is the soul that they must own through identification, not necessarily the body.

This cannot be a sham just to get increased productivity; it must be genuine. That which is **real** will always be the result of real leadership. This is one way the Japanese attained such high levels of productivity from their people; they think of the company they work for as an extension of their own family. The Japanese are more reticent about leaving a company than most Americans are about getting a divorce. The average Japanese worker has forty percent or more of his income directly tied to productivity or profitability. The more a person partakes of the fruit of his own tree (job) the more motivation he will have.

THE COMING CHANGE IN CAPITALISM

In the coming years capitalism is destined to change just as radically as socialism has recently. (This is not to imply that we will become communist; capitalism and communism are not the only options for economic systems.) The change will be as sweeping and profound as the recent changes in Eastern Europe and in the Soviet Union. Those who do not see the changes coming and become part of the new breed of leadership will be swept away by those changes just as the archaic communist leaders were.

There is a difference between free enterprise and capitalism. Within true free enterprise everyone has an equal opportunity; in the present capitalism only those with the capital have an equal opportunity. Even though the multi-level marketing enterprises such as Amway, A.L. Williams, Shaklee, Mary Kay and others, have often been disdained by many of the present powers in American commerce, they have prevailed to become an important and revolutionary new force in business. These companies have built on what will become the most powerful economic engine of the future. Even though the formative stages of some of these businesses may have been built with almost as much hype as clear strategy, they have been economic pioneers who have opened up financial territories possibly no less significant to our future than the opening of the Western frontiers.

Generally, multi-level marketing companies have fielded quality products at good values while rewarding their people many times what they could have made at comparable positions in other companies. This has been done by substantially reducing the high overhead most companies have with administrative bureaucracy and benefits by making each "employee" an independent contractor. By making their employees independent businesses, or franchises, every employee decides his own benefits and bears the costs. The independent business person also directly partakes of the rewards if his business does well, or suffers if it does not, which tends to radically increase productivity. Because he also shares a percentage of each new business he helps get started through sponsorship, competition becomes a positive force instead of a negative one; everyone works to help everyone else do well. Multi-level marketing *is* an economic American revolution which has the potential to impact the world as profoundly as did the first one. Already its accomplishments have been of historic proportions; its future potential is even greater.

Along with emphasizing ownership and direct reward for initiative, these organizations excel in recognizing and building *leadership*. Again, man is territorial; his soul is linked to ownership. In the conflict and pressures of the now changing world it is essential for those in leadership to understand this.

THE LEADERSHIP OF STRATEGIC RETREAT

Because of the reality that any moment may be the last in the midst of a battle, war concentrates and reveals human nature at its most basic level. The Union General Meade has been much criticized by military historians for being indecisive at the Battle of Gettysburg. However, in his situation what seemed to be indecision may have been a brilliant strategy. He did little more than just decide to make a stand. Effective leadership is being able to discern one's position and take *proper* action. Meade may well have discerned after the first day that his troops would not give up any more of *their territory*. They had retreated as far as they would and their position was now stronger because of this. This strategy proved itself as the men who had fled so many times before the brilliant Lee did not give up another acre, even under the most intense pressure they had ever faced.

Retreating from your territory can be demoralizing and disastrous, but on occasion it can be motivating and strategic. When faced with greater odds it is sometimes necessary, but you have to utilize it to increase the fight in your troops instead of allowing it to sap their initiative. Sam Houston used this tactic brilliantly as he retreated before the hated Santa Ana. His proud Texans became increasingly enraged with each mile of Texas they yielded. Santa Ana got cockier and more careless. When it reached a point at which the Texans were either going to fight or string up Houston himself, he turned them loose—it was no contest even though the numbers were still greatly in Santa Ana's favor.

The Russian General Kutuzov and his comparatively little army retreated for almost a thousand miles before Napoleon's hoards. All of Russia, his own generals and even the Czar became distraught. Why did he not at least give a fight? But he resisted the pressure until the time was right for a stand. While he retreated he gathered regiment after regiment from the countryside. Though his army was still not even close to Napoleon's strength, he sensed at Borodino that it was the proper *time*. Moscow was at their back and his men were enraged.

Napoleon began the battle with a cannonade so terrible observers believed that there would be little need for the infantry because there could be little left of the Russians after it. To the astonishment of the French the Russians held their ground. Then Bonaparte sent wave after wave of his previously invincible infantry at the seemingly weak Russian front. Even after his numerous battles it was said that Napoleon became ill at the carnage that day, possibly the bloodiest single day in the history of warfare. Even though the French significantly outnumbered the Russians in everything from cannons to men, they could not move them from their positions. Kutuzov issued no directives that day; he calmly sat and watched, nodding or shaking his head to approve or deny requests made to him. When the sun set that evening and the smoke cleared, Kutuzov still held the field of battle. The French were in dismay. Men will take stands and fight with a will that defies all logic when *their* territory is threatened.

That night as Kutuzov surveyed the carnage he determined to retreat again. Again it was a brilliant strategy. Dozens of generals, thousands of officers, tens of thousands of men, lay scattered on the field. He did not even have enough officers left to give sufficient battle orders. So he withdrew and resolved to fight on with guerilla warfare, the only strategy left available to them, but they did not quit until the French were driven from their land. They would burn their beloved Moscow and its countryside rather than give it to the enemy. When you have touched the soil you have touched the soul.

Historians still argue that, if Kutuzov had just held his position anyway, the French would have retreated. Napoleon was obviously shaken by the Russian resolve at Borodino. Napoleon may have won the battle by attrition, but the victory would cost him the war. Many great leaders in business and enterprise have been defeated by the same type of victory. Sometimes our resolve to advance sets us up for defeat and retreat. On occasion our retreat can be the springboard for an advance. A wise leader will know his people and his territory.

HUMAN EGO AND THE DESTRUCTION OF EMPIRES

Why was Napoleon driven to invade Russia? He had beaten the Czar Alexander in battle before; then they had become friends and allies. Alexander had objected to Napoleon's treatment of a conquered nobleman and that objection insulted Napoleon. Almost a million people had to die because Napoleon was insulted. Napoleon was one of the most remarkable characters in history, one of the most effective leaders of all time, but his pettiness destroyed him. You can be a great leader without being a great man. Great men are not affected or motivated by insults, or the determination to get even with perceived or real unfairness on the part of competitors, regulators, or the public. Negative motivation for retaliation is often the seed of defeat or destruction. As with Napoleon, and Hitler after him, that kind of motivation leads to disastrous decisions.

Conquest can be a positive and a noble motive. It can also be the most evil and empty one. The soul of America is linked to conquest and adventure. Regardless of the accusations, America's motives for conquest have seldom been imperialistic in nature; it has been the result of the desire to achieve, to push back the outer limits. That's why Americans will excel in research, development and exploration, but they become bored with the process of manufacturing. In contrast, the Asians love and are very adept at the tedious labor of manufacturing. Without a vision for conquering, not so much people or lands but limits, America will eventually wither away (American leadership in development and exploration *combined with* Asian management and manufacturing could produce a peerless team). Those who lead Americans politically, economically through business, or spiritually, will have only limited success at best if they are not in some defined way setting their goals to push back the present limits of their time. America was birthed by explorers and adventurers and she still carries their genetic code; that is her soul.

The television miniseries and book "Roots" was popular because almost everyone could identify with the author, Alex Hailey, as he found his identity in his heritage. Our vision of the future will be clarified by our understanding of the past. The soul of a people is identified with the soil, and that soil is not just dirt, it is history. Every nation, people, and even every enterprise has a genetic code that is *spiritual,* which has been set to a large degree by its history. These codes can be affected and changed, but they will not be fully understood until their history is known.

Motivation will directly effect performance, production or the **Product** that is the heart of your venture. Even the noblest goals will not motivate if the people cannot identify with them. Those goals must become their "land." Personal recognition and rewards are important in making the vision real. Progress toward the attainment of goals must touch you in a practical way and affect you positively or the goals will not be real.

Providing a better lifestyle for one's family can be a noble goal. Just getting richer or conquering for the sake of ego will result in increasing emptiness and a deterioration of self-esteem. Unfortunately these have been the only goals of an increasing percentage of Americans for the last few decades. Leadership has not provided other goals worthy of capturing our attention. Except for a few fits and starts the downward slide of American enterprise has been continuous for that same period of time. Only a true leader can provide a true vision that will inspire the people and cause them to identify with it.

There are many forces of philosophy at work in America which discourage the pursuit of leadership. Anyone who takes initiative becomes the target of a destructive criticism from lesser souls; such criticism is designed to pull everyone else down to their level. Much of the media has become the embodiment of the "crab spirit" in humanity. Crabs can be kept in containers from which they could easily escape, but if one starts to rise above his fellows to get out they will pull him back down. With just a little cooperation, they could all escape—but the nature of crabs keeps them all in bondage. In the same fashion, the media, in the name of journalism, has been used to release some of the worst characteristics in men. Pointless, destructive criticism once an anathema is now regarded as a virtue—as the media delights in questioning the motives of even the most trustworthy of leaders.   Many journalists consider anyone who is taking initiative or leadership an easy target.   The result has been a vacuum of leadership that has historically provided an opportunity for a most undesirable type of leader to step into the void.

Chapter Seven

They Changed The Course Of History

The Knights of the Order of St. John, and their exploits during the Middle Ages, are some of the greatest historic examples of what can be accomplished by those who live by the highest standards of leadership. Against odds that some historians have estimated were over one hundred to one, these few knights took their stand against the most powerful armies of Islam and prevailed. Their history is worthy of recounting as one of the great inspirations, and definitions, of true leadership the world has ever produced.

As Christian Europe succumbed to increasing division and internal conflict, the Islamic Ottoman Empire was unifying the Moslem world. Having finally driven the Crusaders from Palestine, Islam turned its attention to the conquest of Europe. Because of the internal conflicts within Europe, there was no one who could raise a Christian army to stand against the hoards from the East. To the Turks, Europe now appeared as an open treasure chest.

In 1309 the few remaining knights of the Order of St. John conquered the island of Rhodes, situated precariously almost within sight of the heart of the Ottoman Empire, but the knights saw it as convenience. The Order quickly began building fortifications, and Rhodean seaman, who for centuries had been the best in the world, taught their skills to the knights. The Order built ships and immediately began to raid Moslem shipping. They quickly made themselves odious to the Ottomans with the boldness of their raids. For the next one hundred and fifty years the Order was so efficient in their sea war that the Turks and Moslems were discouraged from even trying to become a great sea power.

At first these raids were little more than an irritation to the Turks. But as the knights gained experience, they became so efficient and daring that they began to pose a serious threat to the supply lines of the Islamic armies massing to conquer Western Europe.

Then Mehmet became Sultan of the Ottomans, and one of the most distinguished leaders in history. A brilliant man who was fluent in a half dozen languages, and possessed extensive knowledge of literature and science, Mehmet quickly raised the cultural and military excellence of his people to a level which surpassed the great nations of Europe. Becoming irritated with the knights, he determined that he would send a force to eradicate this increasing nuisance.

Even though the monarchs of Europe were glad that the knights were at least distracting the Turks, they scorned them as "archaic relics from the past." When the Order requested supplies and reinforcements to stand against the invading Moslem army, all of Europe refused to help, considering them to be doomed. Still the knights determined not to retreat, accepting death rather than to yield a single acre to the enemies of the cross.

THE FIRST BATTLE OF RHODES

Islam was founded on the theology of *Jihad*, which is a Holy War to conquer the world by force for Allah. War is glorified in Islam, and death in Jihad guaranteed one their place in heaven, regardless of previous sins. When the religious leaders proclaimed a conflict to be a Jihad, the doors of heaven were opened to anyone who gave their life for the cause. Multitudes saw Jihad as their opportunity to gain heaven in spite of their debauchery, so they actually hoped to die in battle. This made the warriors of Islam some of the most deadly and feared that the world had ever seen.

Mehmet was also a conqueror at heart who fashioned himself after Alexander the Great. He marched on the great city of Constantinople, and conquered it. He then set his sights on the rest of Europe. But before he could take the rest of Europe, he had to do something about the annoying knights at Rhodes who continued to plunder his shipping and supply lines.

In 1480 Mehmet sent his most able generals with an army of 70,000 men to subdue the 600 knights and 1,500 to 2,000 militia at Rhodes. Even though the knights were so few, they had proven so capable in previous conflicts that Mehmet wanted to take no chances. It appeared to all that the siege of Rhodes would be brief and decisive.

After landing his army, Mehmet's siege cannons began to batter the walls the Order had spent over a century building. Numerous other cannons hurled projectiles over the walls into the city. The Grand Master of the Order was a Frenchman named D'Aubusson. He was a remarkable leader of men who had with great foresight prepared his knights for the siege he knew would one day come. He even had built shelters for the townspeople so that they could escape the bombardment. Knowing that they could expect little or no help from Europe, D'Aubusson nevertheless had determined that they would stand as long as one knight could draw a bow or wield a sword.

In Early June, after days of bombardment, the first wave of assault troops attacked the Tower of St. Nicholas, an outlying fortification of the city. The Moslems were shocked by the stiff resistance they met, and were repulsed with many casualties. The Turks then began another general bombardment that would hurl over a thousand cannon balls a day at the city continuously for several weeks. The walls began to collapse while the Turks snaked closer and closer with their trenches. At night fires burned everywhere from the grenades and incendiaries. Those who were present declared that a scene out of hell itself could be no worse. Still the knights held their ground.

On June 18, the Turks launched a second human wave assault led by the fearsome Janissaries, renowned as the greatest fighters in the world. Each Janissar had been chosen from age seven because of their physical potential, and trained their entire lives for combat. They had been forbidden to marry or engage in any kind of family affections in order to focus all of their emotions and energy on battle. The assault began under the cover of darkness, when they expected to find the knights sleeping—but they were wrong. Swords, arrows and gunfire filled the night. As the sun rose it revealed legions of Janissar bodies filling the moats around the tower of St. Nicholas, and the knights still standing on the battered walls.

The disbelieving Turkish generals had never experienced such a military setback. They turned to subterfuge to pry the knights from their fortress city. They planted agents in the city by having them pretend to be defectors to the Christians (many of the Sultan's troops were captives from Christian nations). These spies were soon able to create serious tactical problems for the knights, who were now being pressed from within and without. Each day presented a new crisis that threatened their very existence. The fortifications were crumbling everywhere, even at the most strategic points. Still they held on. Then the Turks began massing for a final great assault that both sides fully expected to be the end.

The great attack began on July 27. The knights and the remaining militia took their positions on what was left of the walls. The Sultan sent his Bashi-Bazouk troops first. These were mercenaries who were considered expendable, and they were expended as wave after wave were cut down by the defenders. Their bodies soon filled the ditches and streams making human bridges that led up to the walls, which had in fact been the strategy of the Turkish generals. Then the tired and wounded defenders watched as great waves of the fearsome Janissaries arose and advanced, even more resolute now because of their previous humiliation.

The Turks quickly overwhelmed the strategic Tower of St. Nicholas, which had taken the brunt of the main assault for nearly two months. As promised, the knights contested every acre of ground, for which the Turks paid very dearly. D'Aubusson, with an arrow in his thigh, led a dozen knights and three standard bearers up a ladder and onto the wall. There D'Aubusson received four more wounds before a Janissar "of gigantic structure" hurled a spear right through his breastplate, puncturing his lung. He was dragged out of the fray just as the enemy made a breach in the defenses and began to pour into the city. It now appeared certain that the end of the Knights of St. John had finally come.

In hand to hand combat, over burning rubble, through choking smoke and fire, in possibly the worst hell that men could create for themselves on the earth, the Turks continued to throw themselves against the knights. Even so, the tenacity of the knights, and their ability to inflict casualties, astonished the Turks. Soon even the resolve of the Janissaries was shaken as row after row of men continued to be cut down by the defenders.

Then, above the smoke and turmoil of this terrible inferno, on the one remaining parapet, D'Aubusson's standards suddenly appeared, held by three bearers in shining armor who appeared almost as gods from the hell below. The affect on the Moslems was electrifying as a wave of fear swept through the army. The remaining Bashi began to flee in such a terror that it overcame the Janissaries. The entire Moslem army then began to melt away in confusion, retreating at the very moment when total victory was easily within their grasp.

As the Moslems fled Rhodian sharpshooters on the walls poured a deadly fire into them. The remaining knights amazingly found enough strength to counterattack, chasing the Sultan's troops all the way to their base camp. Within ten days the shattered army that had been the pride of the Ottomans fled the island. To the astonishment of the entire world, the Order of St. John had not only survived—they had prevailed. All of Europe celebrated. All of Islam was enraged.

ISLAM IN CHECK

That decimation of the great army of the seemingly unconquerable Sultan, Mehmet, by such a small force, was viewed as a military miracle of biblical proportions. The Order that had been viewed by Europe as "an archaic relic of the past," was elevated to a new prominence, and was now viewed as the savior of the continent. But the knights wasted little time celebrating; they immediately began to rebuild their fortifications for what they fully expected to be an even greater assault. They were correct in their assessment.

Because of this defeat Islam was in check. They could not advance into Europe with the knights holding Rhodes and threatening their lines of supply. The knights knew that they were now more odious than ever to the Sultan, and that they were now too weakened to endure another assault.

Mehmet raised another, even larger army, but on his way south to attack the Order, the Sultan became sick and died. The knights considered this as great a miracle as their recent victory. Even though they were committed to taking their stand through another siege, they knew they had no chance in any conflict without Divine intervention. Because Mehmet's second expedition against Rhodes was cancelled by his death, the knights were given a little more time to heal their wounds and repair the walls before the next onslaught. Fittingly, even D'Aubusson survived his wounds.

The knights began preparations for the next battle with their characteristic resolve. It was as if they knew that the world's destiny had been cast upon their shoulders. Now money and munitions poured into the tiny island from Europe, and almost all of it was devoted to the reconstruction of the walls and towers. The army of the Crescent would not return to Rhodes for forty years, but it would take that long for the Order to prepare for what was coming.

D'Aubusson died in 1503, but his vision and leadership insured that the fortress would grow even stronger than it had been before the first siege. These efforts were not wasted—an even greater test was coming. Meanwhile, Europe was also being given desperately needed time to regroup.

SULEIMAN ASCENDS

In 1520 "Suleiman The Magnificent" ascended to the throne of the Ottoman Empire. Like Mehmet II, he was a man of culture and learning, as well as a brilliant general. Under his leadership the empire would rise to its greatest heights, and its power was without rival in the world.

One year later, Phillippe Villiers de L'Isle Adam became the Grand Master of the Order Of St. John. L'Isle Adam was likewise an educated aristocrat, as well as an experienced seaman and a devout Christian. He would also prove to be a great leader. The main players for another one of history's most strategic conflicts were now in place.

In 1521 the Sultan sent the newly elected Grand Master "A Letter Of Victory," in which he boasted of his recent victories and asked that the Grand Master "rejoice with me over my triumphs." L'Isle Adam was more direct than diplomatic; he replied that he fully understood the meaning of the letter—that Suleiman intended to make Rhodes his next conquest.

In his next letter the Sultan demanded that Rhodes be surrendered to him at once. The Sultan's timing was typically brilliant. Henry VIII of England was in the process of seizing the Order's rich properties in Britain. France and Spain were at war, and Italy was already devastated. Again, the Order could expect no help or reinforcements. A few hundred gallant knights would again have to stand alone against the most powerful army on earth.

THE SECOND BATTLE OF RHODES

By June 1522 Suleiman was ready for his assault on Rhodes. Historians estimate that the Sultan assembled up to 700 ships and 200,000 men for the attack. Even allowing for natural exaggeration, this was an overwhelming force to come against 500 knights and an estimated 1,500 militia. On July 28, the Sultan himself landed on Rhodes with a grand salute and the battle began.

The Turks brought up their huge siege guns, capable of hurling balls nine feet in circumference, along with a multitude of other cannons and mortars to begin their bombardment. Throughout the month of August they poured thousands of cannon balls into the city and its fortified positions each day. The knights answered with their own artillery, much smaller, but devastatingly accurate on the relatively unprotected Turks.

By the end of August, a number of breeches began to appear in the fortress walls. In early September the first infantry assault came. Typically, the knights contested every point, but the overwhelming numbers pushed back the defenders until the Turks were able to plant their standards on the wall itself. Never had the knights lost that much ground in the first attack. They counterattacked with the Grand Master himself entering the fray. After a terrible struggle the Turks yielded and began to fall back. Immediately the Sultan sent a second wave, personally led by Mustapha Pasha, one of the greatest Ottoman generals. For two hours the battle raged on the walls, but the knights held. When the Turks finally withdrew, the ground was almost completely covered by their dead and wounded. Miraculously, the knights had lost only three dead along with an unspecified number of militia.

The disconcerted Sultan then unleashed a continuous bombardment for three straight weeks. On September 24 another great assault was hurled against the crumbling fortress walls. The bastion of Aragon, one of the city's main fortifications, fell to a massive assault by the now fanatically brave Janissaries, having born the humiliation from their previous defeat for over forty years. Like Xerxes, Suleiman had a conqueror's throne set on a raised platform so that he could witness his day of triumph. The tide of battle roared all along the walls as wave after wave of Turks poured out of their trenches.

All day long the battle continued to rage. The knights, in their gleaming armor, always seemed to appear wherever the fighting was the thickest. L'Isle Adam himself could usually be found with his standard bearer behind him at the most desperate points of conflict. He was the man the Turks most wanted killed, and his standard bearer seemed to mark him as the special target. Yet, it was witnessed by those present that there was a special protection around the Grand Master that the Turks simply could not penetrate. After one of the bloodiest days the great Turkish army would ever experience, the seemingly invincible attack began to waver, then melt into a wholesale retreat.

The disbelieving Suleiman came down from his elevated throne humiliated and outraged. He immediately condemned his two most able generals, but later recanted after being persuaded that it would only serve the side of the Christians. The losses for the knights had been great, with two hundred killed and an equal number wounded, but the losses for the Turks were staggering—their bodies now laid in heaps all around the city. Again, the great siege guns were brought up and would not fall silent again for two entire months.

The gallant knights had stood their ground against the most powerful and determined army on earth for nearly five months without receiving reinforcements or provisions. They were now few and weary, and it was obvious to all that the Turkish army was still so huge that it would eventually prevail. Still they fought on, their greatest hope now was only to die honorably.

THE SULTAN'S BENEVOLENCE

As the siege wore on, the Sultan's disposition toward the Order gradually began to change. He respected honor and courage, and had never witnessed the kind of valor that these brave knights had displayed. On Christmas Eve, Suleiman made an extraordinary offer of peace with honor to the remaining knights. He paid tribute to their courage and endurance. He gave them provisions and his own ships to carry them to the destination of their choice. After meeting with L'Isle Adam, Suleiman is reported to have said to his Grand Vizir, "It saddens me to be compelled to force this brave old man to leave his home."

Two thousand men had taken their stand against as many as two hundred thousand, and had held their ground for over six months. They endured possibly the greatest bombardment and infantry assaults that the world had seen until that time. When hearing the news of the final fall of Rhodes, Charles V of France stated that, "Nothing in the world was ever so well lost as Rhodes." The knights who had already gained the respect of the entire world, were esteemed even more. Even so, some of the greatest exploits of the Order were yet to come.

THE KNIGHTS OCCUPY MALTA

For over two hundred years the knights had lived on Rhodes and now they had no home. They were offered a small, relatively inhospitable island in the middle of the Mediterranean named Malta, which they accepted. Years before, while harbored on a ship at Malta, lightening had struck the sword of L'Isle Adam, turning it to ashes. This was to be considered a Providential sign. The knights were destined to fight yet another one of history's most strategic battles on the bluffs around that very harbor.

With Rhodes in his possession, the Sultan now seemed free to sweep up the rest of Europe. It must have seemed most improbable that the battered knights would again bar his path. Though the Order of St. John was severely reduced in both numbers and wealth after their departure from Rhodes, their most valuable possession— resolve—was as great as ever.

Christian Europe had not only failed to resolve its internal divisions, the Reformation had caused even further conflicts. Centuries of resentment toward Rome boiled over into wars as Christians took up arms against each other. Almost every nation in Europe was at war to some degree with at least one neighbor.

The Order of St. John itself was composed of knights from the noble families of every Christian nation, but somehow they were able to maintain a remarkable unity. They remained focused on what they considered to be the real enemy of the faith—the hoards of Islam.

As soon as the knights occupied Malta, they began building fortifications and ships so that they could resume raiding Moslem shipping. The famous Arab pirate, Barbarossa, had been appointed High Admiral of the Turkish fleet, and he raised its quality and strength to new heights. Great sea battles raged from one end of the Mediterranean to the other. Though most of these battles were indecisive they kept the world on the edge of its seat.

In 1546 Barbarossa died and Dragut assumed command of the increasingly powerful Turkish navy. In 1550 the knights were major participants in the defeat of his fleet at Mahdia. For revenge, Dragut attacked and began to lay waste to Malta. Still relatively unfortified, the few defenders put up such a stiff resistance that Dragut abandoned the attack, but both sides knew that the Turks would soon return.

In 1557 L'Isle Adam died and Jean Parisot De La Valette became Grand Master of the Order. Also educated and aristocratic, La Valette was once captured by the Turks and had been made a galley slave for four years. He was sixty-three when he became Grand Master. He would prove to be as great a leader as both L'Isle Adam and d'Aubusson had been before him. Suleiman had now stretched his empire to its greatest limits and was massing for what appeared to be the final assault on Europe. But again the knights had to be dealt with because they were creating such havoc with his supply lines, although they were fewer in numbers and farther away.

THE BATTLE OF MALTA

The whole Moslem world was also demanding the destruction of the Order of St. John. The Sultan was ambivalent. At times he was enraged at the knights, and at times he feared them, knowing that they could not be defeated without great cost. Public opinion soon forced his hand and on May 18, 1565, the Turkish fleet was sighted by the watchman in Fort St. Elmo on the edge of Malta.

The Moslem fleet was so large that witnesses said that it appeared as if an entire forest of spars were moving across the Mediterranean. In fact, the world had never witnessed a more powerful fleet assembled. Again, tens of thousands of the Sultan's finest Janissaries, regulars, and over 4,000 Iayalars, religious fanatics who sought death over life, landed to give battle to the 540 knights, 1,000 foot soldiers and a little over 3,000 Maltese militia.

Again the Order faced impossible odds, and never had the Moslems been more determined. The knights did not have enough men to try to hold the invaders at their beachhead. However, unlike Rhodes where there was just one fortified city, at Malta the knights were spread out over several forts and fortified cities that forced the Turks to diversify their forces. La Valette quickly proved to be a genius at taking the maximum advantage of every favorable condition. He sent the Order's cavalry to attack and harass the Turkish foraging parties, which they did to the point of distraction, further disrupting the unity of Moslem forces.

The Turkish High Command was led by the brilliant Mustapha Pasha, but he made a strategic mistake of concentrating his main attack on the Post of Castile, possibly the strongest of the knight's defenses. This was the result of the bravery of a single knight, a Frenchman named Adrien de la Riviere, who had been captured early in the assault. Under torture, de la Riviere had asserted that Post of Castile was lightly fortified with a small garrison of men, and could be easily taken. After a number of assaults were repulsed and mauled by the Post of Castile's defenders, Pasha realized that he had been lied to by the captured knight. He had the Frenchman beaten to death, but he had already lost hundreds of his fighters and even more importantly, his troops had already begun to lose confidence.

THE COURAGE OF ST. ELMO

Then Pasha redirected the main part of his force to capturing the small star fort, St. Elmo, which overlooked the Grand Harbor. This diversion gave La Valette time to make improvements in his other fortifications, but it was apparent that St. Elmo could not hold out long. The indiscriminate gunfire of the Turk's earlier sieges at Rhodes had now been replaced by mathematical precision and accuracy. Pasha turned his main artillery on St. Elmo with unrelenting intensity day and night. Soon the little fort began to crumble.

One night, while in his counsel chamber in Fort St. Angelo, La Valette was disturbed by an unwelcome delegation. A number of knights had slipped out of St. Elmo and made their way to La Valette to tell him that St. Elmo could no longer hold out. La Valette, a hero at Rhodes, derided the younger knights as unworthy of their fathers. He told the delegation that they need not go back to St. Elmo, but that he would hand pick a delegation to relieve them. Under this scorn the delegation from St. Elmo begged to be allowed to return to their post, which La Valette finally permitted. As soon as they had departed, the Grand Master told the council that he knew that the little fort was doomed, but they had to buy more time if the rest were to have any chance to survive.

The Turks had now concentrated so much artillery on St. Elmo that the smoke and fire rising from the fort made it appear like a volcano rising out of the rock. It seemed impossible that anyone could live in it, but the young knights held their ground. Then the famed Dragut arrived with a fresh squadron of ships and hand picked fighting men. This greatly raised the morale of the entire Turkish force.

Dragut unofficially assumed personal command of the forces, and he immediately sent even more batteries to pour their deadly fire into St. Elmo, which he continued for three more weeks. Finally he released the Janissaries to make their attack. The commanders on both sides, who had been certain that Turks would make it a quick victory, were equally astonished when they were repulsed with great losses.

The enraged Dragut then responded with a bombardment so heavy that the entire island shook as if by an earthquake. The next day he sent a second massive assault against the little fort with the Iayalars preceding the Janissaries. St. Elmo actually disappeared under the cloud of dust, smoke and fire. Hours later when the smoke cleared, the knights on St. Angelo and St. Michaels marvelled as they saw the Cross of St. John still flying above the crumbled ruins. La Valette was so moved he dispatched some of his best fighters to reinforce the little fort, but the Moslem forces encircling it could not be penetrated and they had to turn back. The brave little garrison at St. Elmo was now abandoned to its own fate.

The following day Dragut intensified the bombardment of St. Elmo. There were now fewer than 100 knights left in the fort and nearly all were wounded. When the bombardment stopped, the Imams were heard calling the faithful to either conquer or die for Islam. Wave after wave of the best fighters in the Sultan's army threw themselves at the demolished walls of the fort. The remaining knights took their stand in the breach; those who were too weak to stand asked to be carried into the fray so that they could confront the "infidels" one last time. The little fortress that no one believed could hold out more than a day or two, stood for over a month, buying precious time for the rest of the knights to strengthen their other defenses. Little St. Elmo also deprived the Sultan of thousands of his best fighting men, many of his leaders, including the master gunner, the Aga of the Janissaries, and most importantly, Dragut himself, felled by a cannon shot.

As the Moslem standard was finally raised over the ruins of St. Elmo, Pasha realized that his whole strategy had been wrong. The price paid for St. Elmo had been too dear. As he looked up at the larger St. Angelo, whose guns were already pouring a deadly fire into his advancing troops, he cried out, "Allah! If so small a son has cost so dear, what price shall we have to pay for so large a father?" The price would be greater than he could afford.

No Quarter Will Be Given

Pasha had the bodies of the knights who had died so bravely at St. Elmo, decapitated, bound to crosses, and floated out into the harbor in front of St. Angelo. This was a brazen insult to the religion of the defenders. In retaliation La Valette had a number of the Turkish prisoners executed and their bodies hung on the walls. He then had their heads loaded into cannons and fired into the Moslem trenches. Both sides now knew that there could be no turning back—the knights would survive on Malta or they would perish to a man—this was a fight to the death.

The bombardments increased as the Order's fortresses were now caught in a deadly crossfire. Intermittently, Pasha would release his massive ground assaults at different points of the defenses, seeking just a single breach. Each one resulted in a massacre of his forces. At one point Pasha maneuvered his troops until they encircled La Valette's own headquarters. He then released a bombardment so great that the inhabitants of the islands of Syracuse and Catania, 70 and 100 miles away, heard the roar of the guns. Before the guns had even stopped Pasha sent a colossal attack swarming over the walls. The Turks finally made a breach and poured into it. A mighty struggle raged for six hours until the knights closed the gap and retook the walls. Mortified, Pasha pulled out his own beard and called off the attack. Again, the endurance and tenacity of the knights had been greatly underestimated.

ANOTHER MIRACLE

Pasha intensified his bombardment and continued it day and night for seven more days. Then he released another human wave assault. By now the Order was so reduced in numbers that the breach was made quickly. The knights resisted bravely but they were too outnumbered to stand against so great a tide of raging humanity. Just when the citadel itself was within reach of the Turks, and it appeared once again that the end of the knights had finally come, the Moslem trumpets rang out calling for a full scale retreat!

The defenders could only believe that the continent had finally sent them relief. What in fact happened was that a small force of the Order's cavalry had attacked the Moslem base camp at Marsa. The little detachment had struck with such determination and had raised so much havoc that they had been mistaken for a much larger force. Fearing an attack from the rear, Pasha had been forced to call a retreat. When he finally learned how he had been deceived right at the very moment when victory was within his grasp, his rage knew no bounds. He redoubled his efforts and released a continuous day and night bombardment under which it seemed impossible for any living thing to survive.

No RETREAT

The council of knights recommended that a withdrawal be made from all of the outposts into the single fortress of St. Angelo. La Valette adamantly refused. They were bound by honor not to willingly surrender an acre to the infidels. Military historians agree that his tenacity in holding to this strategy probably saved the knights, because it kept the Turks from massing at a single point. La Valette received a dispatch from Don Garcia of Sicily promising to send a relief force of 16,000 men. La Valette was unimpressed. Having received many such promises before, he did not put his trust in princes. He vowed to continue to contest every parcel of Christian ground before he would surrender it to the Turks.

Pasha had not only been pouring their deadly fire into the city over its walls, he had been spending weeks making tunnels under the walls. On August 18, a mine exploded under the Post of Castile and a great breach was made. The Grand Master himself, now seventy years old, grabbed a light helmet and his sword and rushed out boldly to meet the attack. The knights and the townspeople, encouraged by his example, picked up any weapon that they could find and flung themselves into the breach with him. La Valette was wounded but refused to retreat. He pointed his sword at the Turkish banners and declared, "Never will I withdraw as long as those banners wave in the wind." Miraculously the knights again prevailed, and the Turks were repulsed.

By now dissensions began to arise within the ranks of the Turkish High Command. The battle that had been projected to take no more than a few days had lasted months, and still there was no end in sight. Pasha started calculating how he could get enough supplies from Tripoli, Greece, or Constantinople to keep up the siege through the winter.

VICTORY

Then, on September 6, Don Garcia's fleet arrived with 8,000 reinforcements for the knights. Even though 8,000 was not a significant number compared to the still huge army of the Turks, their impact on the morale of both sides was much greater than their numbers. The Turks were simply appalled when they considered what just a few hundred knights had cost them. They had still only captured the tiny fort of St. Elmo; how could they possibly prevail against so many more? Pasha quickly lifted the siege, struck camp, and fled the island.

The Sultan's mighty army returned to the Golden Horn with less than one third of those who had left. Suleiman was again enraged. He only allowed his fleet to come into the harbor under the cover of darkness so that the people would not see its terrible state. He immediately planned to lead another expedition to Malta the following year, but like Mehmet before him, Suleiman would not live to fulfill this vow.

EUROPE CELEBRATES

Only about 250 knights survived on Malta, and almost every one of them was wounded, maimed, or crippled for life, but Europe was now free of the Moslem threat that had so recently appeared invincible. Again the whole world stood in wonder at the little Order of St. John the Baptist. Those "archaic relics from the past" had taken their stand against the greatest army in the world, and with some of the greatest examples of courage and endurance the world had ever witnessed, they had prevailed. The great nations of Europe, which had once scorned the knights, acknowledged that these few brave souls had saved them from Moslem conquest.

In England, where Henry VIII had confiscated the knight's property, Queen Elizabeth declared that if Malta had fallen to the Turks, then England itself would have almost certainly fallen to the Moslems. She ordered the Archbishop of Canterbury to appoint a special form of thanksgiving to be read in every church in the land every day for three weeks. The rest of Europe also celebrated, paid their respects, and acknowledged their debt to the Order that most had long before written off as having no real value. The Order's standard with the famous Maltese Cross would become, for a time, the only standard to be saluted by every nation in the world. Some nations still observe St. John's Day to celebrate the exploits of these valiant knights.

THE LESSONS

There are many great and timely lessons in the amazing history of the Order of St. John, but here we will only address the most basic. Great strategists have often changed the course of history, but these knights were not great strategists—they were simply great souls. Their resolve, courage, and endurance accomplished what possibly no great strategy could have. Sometimes leadership is reduced to just this, and in this leadership often finds its greatest definition. Immature leadership will always be overly focused on the odds, or the resources available. Great leaders are focused on the task. To the greatest leaders, retreat or defeat are not even possibilities.

While the Christian nations of Europe had turned their armies against each other, the knights of St. John stayed focused on who the real enemy was. Even though the Order was composed of the noble sons of those Christian nations that were fighting each other, they did not allow the doctrinal or political divisions to enter their ranks. Because of their unity, focused vision, and determination never to retreat before their enemies, they dramatically turned back what had appeared to be the inevitable course of history. It is now almost impossible to imagine what history would have been like without these few brave souls.

THE PRESENT STATUS OF THE ORDER

The Order's resiliency and ability to survive is almost as amazing as their great military exploits. It is today possibly the only true chivalrous order in existence that has maintained legitimate, continuous roots to the Crusades. Committed to honor, the defense of the faith, Christian unity, and service to "my lords the sick and the poor," the "knights of Malta" as they are now called, are still involved in some of the most extraordinary diplomatic breakthroughs of recent times, albeit without fanfare or any attempts to be recognized.

Just like the church, there are now both Protestant and Catholic divisions of the Order, with some natural contention between them as to which are the true heirs. If the right of survivorship test had to be passed, then The Sovereign Order of St. John the Baptist, of Jerusalem, Rhodes and Malta would win, because the Catholic Order became dormant until resuscitated and a Grand Mastership was recognized by Pope Leo XIII in 1879.

Because both the Protestant and Catholic do have legitimate and substantial claims to the Order's history, both are recognized in many nations. The Catholic Grand Master holds the rank of Cardinal in the church. Protestant Branches of the Order now exist in Canada, Ireland, Germany, Sweden, France, Rhodes, Austria, Switzerland, Belgium, Portugal, Spain, Italy and The Netherlands. A few Americans are represented in both the Catholic and Protestant Orders. Entry into the order can only be attained by recommendation and then qualification, but to become one of the "knights of Malta" is considered by many to be one of the greatest honors in Christendom.

Chapter Eight

The Five Essentials

There are Five Basic Essentials required for success in any enterprise. Whether it is a business, charity, sports team, government, church, mission, the military or even managing a household, understanding and applying these five basic Essentials is a key to solid, secure success. These Essentials are:

- The Product
- Administration
- Marketing
- Resources
- Timing

These five basic Essentials must be understood and combined to work in harmony and support of each other. Failure to understand, control, and keep these essentials in proper balance is a common reason for almost every failure in the history of human enterprise.

THE BALANCE

We can have any four of these Essentials working perfectly but if the other one is ineffective it can destroy the entire venture. For example, we can have a quality **Product**, perfect **Timing** for its release, great **Administration**, plenty of **Resources**, but poor **Marketing** can make all of our efforts fruitless. One can have the perfect **Product, Administration, Timing** and **Marketing**, and a lack of **Resources** can be our doom. To combine any four of the essentials successfully but neglect the other one will put us in jeopardy of ultimate failure.

Once we understand these Five Essentials it is easy to comprehend why the majority of new businesses fail in their first two years of existence. Of those which survive that long, only a fraction will survive three more years. Many great new Products never succeed in the marketplace simply because they were not backed by strength in just one of these five basic Essentials. Of those that do survive, many just limp along, falling short of their real potential, simply because they do not get these basics under control and functioning properly.

Our goal in this study is to impart basic principles which can be understood and applied quickly and easily. Once we understand the mechanics and interrelationship of these Five Essentials, the effectiveness of management will be greatly enhanced.

MANAGING FOR RESULTS

The goal of effective management should always be clarity and simplicity which gets *results*. The gravitation toward esoteric management principles and theories is often nothing more than a cloak for the basic lack of understanding by those who generate them. With few exceptions the greatest leaders and most effective managers have all been committed to understanding and applying the *basics* in their field of enterprise.

Commitment to excellence will only go as deep as our commitment to the philosophy of excellence. Only when we do the right things for the right reasons will our commitment be deep enough to accomplish our potential for true and lasting success. Consequently, the philosophy as well as the practical application of these principles must be considered.

With just a basic understanding of the application of the Five Essentials, we can quickly and effectively discern, and possibly compensate for, weakness in one or more of the other Essentials for a period of time. A weakness in a competitor or enemy can also be easily discerned in this way. The goal of our understanding must be to have all of the Essentials working in harmony like a finely tuned machine, while being able to judge weakness, or opportunity, so that these strengths can be used effectively. To give a brief illustration of how easy it is to analyze almost any project, mission or enterprise, with the Five Essentials, let's use them to superficially dissect three entirely different enterprises: a professional football team, an army and a business.

MANAGING A TEAM

With the football team the game would be its Product. If it can produce a quality game it has a quality Product. The coaching and front office would be the Administration. Marketing would be all of the efforts to promote attendance at the games, an interest in the sport, etc. Resources would be the talent of the players and staff, as well as the capital required to acquire them. *Timing is the fundamental essential which is vital for the success of all of the other Essentials.*

For the football team the proper use of Timing is quite obvious in the game (Product), calling the right plays at the right time, etc., but it is just as essential in every other department. Promotions will be most effective if released in early fall when people start thinking about football; they may have little effect if released in early spring when people start thinking about the lazy days of summer and the more appropriate laidback game of baseball. Administration will have the consideration of Timing as the basis for making most of its decisions. For example, knowing the age and health of their present players should determine *when* they should draft or recruit players for those positions. A continually successful team will be strong and consistent in all five of the Essentials.

Using the Five Essentials to discern the strengths and weaknesses of other teams can play a big part in our team's strategy and planning as well. Knowing that our competitor's Product is strong in pass defense but weak in running defense may cause us to consider giving more attention to our running game to exploit their weakness and avoid their strengths. If our main competition is weak in capitalization, we might need to consider beating them by outbidding them for the quality free agents. Knowing our strengths and weaknesses, as well as those of the competition, will enable us to formulate a more effective strategy.

MANAGING AN ARMY

Now let's look at the army. Its ability to give battle would be its Product. Its Administration would include the commanding general down to the corporal directing a squad. Marketing would be its ability to recruit and maintain public opinion to encourage the civilian sacrifice required for success (Marketing had as much to do with the Allied victory in World War II as field strategy). Its Resources would be the men, arms and supplies available. Timing would be involved in knowing when to attack where and with what weapons, as well as when and how to strengthen certain defenses.

Near the end of World War II, the German army still had a quality Product (ability to fight), good Administration, effective Marketing in promoting the sacrifice required by their population, and almost perfect Timing in initiating the Battle of the Bulge—but the lack of Resources (they ran out of fuel) sealed their defeat. The Allied army's discernment of this German weakness helped them implement a successful defensive strategy. They simply let the Germans advance until their fuel ran out (which created the *bulge*), exploiting this weakness until they attained the ultimate victory.

History testifies that it is poor Timing to invade Russia unless you can get your army out before the winter. Napoleon invaded Russia with overwhelming strength in every Essential except Timing. Even though the French had adequate Resources when they initiated the invasion, their Timing opened a door of vulnerability to the discerning Russians. They could not beat Napoleon on the battlefield so they burned their cities and fields to deprive him of the Resources he was counting on to survive the winter. Through this strategy of attacking the only area of Napoleon's weakness the Russians utterly destroyed one of the most invincible armies ever assembled.

MANAGING A BUSINESS

In considering a business, its Product would be the product(s), or service(s), that it offers. Its Administration would be the management from its board of directors down to the most junior foreman. Marketing would include its promotions and distribution. Resources would include its capitalization, the necessary people, machines, or factories, as well as whatever natural resources are needed to make the Product. Again, Timing is the hub around which the other spokes are joined. We could build the best quality and least expensive hula hoop ever made but if we did not get it out in the 1950's we probably missed our chance.

Piper and Cessna aircraft manufacturers built comparable Products. Both companies had good Administration, adequate Resources and good Timing for their Products. Everything else being about equal, Cessna sold many times the number of aircraft that Piper did simply because they were stronger in Marketing.

Ford Motor Company started off with the best Product, Timing, Resources and Marketing, but was a little weak in

Administration. General Motors started with strength in Administration but was behind in the other Essentials. At first GM could do little more than copy Ford products and patiently wait for Ford to make a mistake. Ford left an opening in Product development and Timing. Ford produced the same Model T year after year while GM started improving their product each year. Through strong Marketing GM made new cars a fad and Ford's Product obsolete, thereby seizing the initiative in the automotive industry which they would not relinquish for decades. Had Ford been monitoring all of the Five Essentials in his enterprise, along with those of his competitor, he would never have fallen behind GM. Had GM been monitoring the Five Essentials in its enterprise, along with its competitor's, it probably would not have lost its leadership to the Japanese, which discerned the trend toward the smaller size and higher quality long before Detroit perceived it.

These are just cursory examples of how an enterprise can be dissected into the Five Essential parts to be more quickly and effectively examined for its strengths and weaknesses. Of course, there will be some variations to these Essentials in every different enterprise. However, generally these principles will be applicable and useful in developing and managing almost any venture.

SPINNING PLATES

There will be a constant shifting of emphasis to shore up one or more of these Five Essentials to maintain a balance in those enterprises that survive and prosper. For example, when major corporations make a change in their Chief Executive Officer, the board will most often use the change to strengthen the Essentials which are showing weakness. If Marketing is soft they will bring in someone strong in that area. However, those in marketing will often have little understanding of engineering or product development, so the Product may tend to suffer while the main emphasis is on Marketing. With the next change they then will bring someone in to strengthen the weakened Product, and the Marketing may begin to weaken again. Seldom is there to be found an enterprise that maintains constant harmony in all of the essential areas. Like clowns spinning plates at the circus—they get one group going and the others start to wobble.

Even so, with a better understanding of these basics it is possible to have all of the essentials doing well at the same time. For a truly healthy and lasting enterprise this is crucial. Many businesses that have failed would not have done so if they had understood and applied these principles. Some may have closed, understanding that their time was over, but they could have been closed in victory instead of defeat and ruin.

Understanding these simple principles can lay a solid foundation for insight and foresight, both of which are necessary for success. In the following chapters we will draw from many different enterprises for examples. This is to help instill creativity in the application of this principle so that you can easily apply it to your own situation.

SIMPLICITY IN DIVERSITY

If we have insight, with a little imagination we can literally see how Napoleon's battle plans will help us in the shop or on the farm. Our situation at the factory or at the law firm may sometimes require just as much courage, determination and brilliance as the most celebrated coaches if we are going to succeed. The basics for all of us are essentially the same. They apply to the largest corporation, government or to the smallest individual proprietor.

Napoleon used the principle of the Five Essentials in all of his military planning. He measured his army's fighting strategies and improved them (the Product). He trained his officers to think strategically, and motivated them with his own vision (Administration). He was a master at raising needed capital, troops and supplies (Resources). His vision and leadership inspired France and sometimes even the citizens of enemy nations (Marketing), and he consistently used Timing as one of his most powerful weapons. He failed only when he neglected one of these essentials.

Captain Rostrom's demonstration of leadership and preparedness as captain of the Carpathia during the Titanic tragedy was aided by his mastery of the Five Essentials. He knew his Product well (the ship). He knew and used his Administration and Resources brilliantly. He was a master of Timing and he conveyed his plan so well (Marketing) that his passengers and crew were utterly focused on the task. He knew his ship and his team well enough to quickly and effectively analyze his limitations and possibilities in the midst of changing circumstances and crisis.

General Lee's use of the Five Essentials while commanding the Army of Northern Virginia is a profound study in this theme. He was able to take full advantage of the Essentials which were strong to overcome those that were weak. He used a fundamental understanding of this principle to know his opponents better than they knew themselves. This kind of insight is both a gift and a discipline to be developed. "You can't put in what God has left out," but we must also develop what God has put in or we have "buried our talents" just as He warned.

An entire volume could easily be devoted to each of these Essentials, but for the sake of brevity and simplicity we will take only a chapter with each. We are not trying to be comprehensive, just effective in imparting easy-to-use principles that work. Using the Five Essentials can aid us in being prepared with the necessary knowledge; but *leadership* is required to implement this knowledge properly.

Chapter Nine

The Product

THE MORAL IMPORTANCE OF THE PRODUCT

The Product is the REASON for the enterprise; it is what we *produce*. The Product can be a commodity, a service, even an idea, but it must be kept as the reason for the enterprise. If anything supplants the Product as the primary reason for the enterprise, at that point the slide into mediocrity or failure will begin.

Profit is what usually supplants the Product as the reason for the enterprise. This is not to say that profit should not be *a* motive for the venture, but it should never be *the* motive. Detroit ruled the automotive world when it was motivated by a love for cars. When the finance men gained control of Detroit and changed the emphasis to profit, American leadership in that industry began its decline. These men were needed by the industry to increase efficiency, but it was a mistake to allow them to take control. They reduced a great art to mere manufacturing, and "mere manufacturing" is contrary to the soul of America.

America's soul is linked closely to conquest and adventure. This is not an imperialistic type of conquest; it is more the desire to achieve, to push back the outer limits. Without a vision for conquering limits we become bored and our performance falls. Americans will excel at manufacturing only if the process somehow identifies the enterprise with breaking new barriers, not just fattening the bottom line. Profit alone is a superficial and uninspiring goal to the work force, which is itself a critical key to success.

MAINTAINING OUR FIRST LOVE

Henry Ford may have impacted the world as much as any other man in modern history; he advanced manufacturing to the point where the modernization that has swept the world was possible. His vision was fired by a love for the car and the desire to make it cheaper and available to more people. But Henry Ford fell from grace—soon he was more captivated by the process of making the car than the car itself. He kept tweaking the assembly line to make it faster and more efficient, and we all benefitted from this, *but he forgot to continue improving the car.*

General Motors easily copied Ford's manufacturing improvements but also strove to make better cars. Little, unknown GM quickly surpassed Ford and for a very long time dominated the industry. GM did not forget why they were in manufacturing, at least until the accountants gained control. When you lose your first love you have stopped the process of growing and started the process of dying.

We may be a manufacturer of the most mundane, insignificant widget there is, but we must not ever think of it as such. If it is worth making it is important, worth being proud of, and it *can be* an inspiration to our people. Remember Martin Luther King's exhortation, "We must do everything that we do like it is the most important job in the world. If we sweep streets then we must sweep streets like Michelangelo painted. If you're the best at what you do, even if it's sweeping streets, the whole world will beat a path to your door and declare that 'Here lives the best street sweeper that ever lived.'" As King Solomon put it, "The skilled craftsman will not stand before obscure men, but will sit in the presence of kings." It does not matter what you do; if you do it with all of your heart, day in and day out, you will inspire those around you, and there is little that can prevent you from rising to the top.

Regardless of how good your product is and how well it beats the competition, if you are always seeking to improve it, you are sending a powerful message to every little corner of your enterprise. This attitude can do more for affecting company loyalty than fat bonuses.

Every individual's job is his own personal Product. Every Product must be esteemed as important because that makes every person important. This means more to them than just about anything else you can offer. If every individual's Product is important then the overall Product of the enterprise is that much more so. Regardless of your position in the enterprise, faithfulness to this concept ensures your success and makes you a true leader. If you are a leader and your enterprise is composed of leaders, your Product is almost assured of leading its field.

TWO GREAT LEADERS

When I was learning the carpenter trade I had the privilege of working with a great craftsman we knew simply as "Old Joe." At that time the country was in a severe recession. One day I remarked how so many in our trade were being hurt by it. He objected, declaring that "No good carpenters are ever hurt by recession." He saw recessions as bringing a healthy pruning of the trade, an opportunity to purge the pretenders.

This old man had been through the depression and a multitude of recessions and hardly knew that they were happening because he built houses like Michelangelo painted frescoes. He took three young men and inspired such a love for carpentry in us that we were disappointed to see five o'clock come each day because it meant we had to stop. At night we couldn't wait for the next morning so we could get started again. We did great work but we were always trying to do even better.

I have known a few important business, political and church leaders, but few ever impressed me as much as that old carpenter. I will always remember him as a great man and a great leader. His Product made him great. Every man is ultimately known by his Product. Is this not what Jesus meant when He said, "By their fruits you will know them"? Every man is ultimately known by what he produces and leaves behind.

A few years later I became a flight instructor and I considered myself one of the great American pilots. I then met a pilot named Joe Logan. He owned North American Aircraft Delivery and was a world renowned aircraft ferry pilot. He had flown over one hundred small, single engine aircraft across the Atlantic and on to such places as Saudi Arabia and South Africa. Israel, who was considered to have some of the best military pilots in the world, once actually hired Joe to train some of theirs.

Even so, in my typical, foolish arrogance, on my first flight with Joe I determined that I was going to teach him a few things about flying. We were hardly off the ground before he was in my face screaming about my lack of smoothness and then he seized the controls. As I watched him I soon felt that I did not even deserve to be a private pilot, much less a commercial pilot and flight instructor! I had never seen such precision and knowledge of the air and the aircraft. I went on to train pilots for their airline ratings, and worked with some who were considered top fighter pilots, but I never met another one as good as Joe. One day he shared his secret with me.

Ferrying aircraft meant dozens of hours of almost unbearable boredom, occasionally interrupted by a few brief moments of sheer terror. Joe determined on one of his first flights that he was not going to just sit there and watch the gauges while the autopilot did all the work—he was going to use this time to become the best pilot that he could.

Joe flew those missions by hand and he kept score on himself. He would put a clipboard in the cockpit, and whenever he deviated from the course more than five degrees, or from his altitude by more than fifty feet, or even slightly felt any "G" forces during a maneuver indicating a lack of precision, he put a mark on the board. The first few times when he reached his destination he would have several hundred marks on the board. Most pilots would consider that a great score under the circumstances. Many pilots would have considered it a great score just to get there! Joe determined that every time he got in the cockpit he was going to improve his score. On one of his last trips he had just two marks on the board and he still was not satisfied! No one knew or cared about this but Joe. He was determined to be the best pilot that he could be.

YOUR PRODUCT IS YOU

Your Product is an extension of your soul, it is a reflection of who you are. If you run a large corporation then everything it does is You. If you run a small shop by yourself, your work is You. If you are the assistant to the janitor, you can inspire everyone in the company by your devotion to excellence. If you are a housewife you can instill greatness and a focused leadership vision in your whole family by how you manage your home. There is a great biblical truth which states—*you will reap what you sow*. If you are tireless in doing the best you can do you will ultimately be rewarded.

THE FOUNDATION OF GREATNESS

A fundamental reason for the early failure of business is that many go into business just to be their own boss. That is not a good reason for starting an enterprise and will seldom provide the motivation to endure the problems and obstacles required to succeed. There is something in most of us that rebels at the thought of just being average. Those who are not striving to rise above the status quo usually spend most of their free time dreaming about it. However, if we really want our lives to be significant the delusion must be dispelled that seeking greatness will ever make us great. With but a few exceptions, those who have left their imprint on human history did so because they were focused on something beyond themselves—they were focused on the Product.

Those who just seek greatness are self-centered. When the self-centered and self-important gain influence or power they become the tyrants and scourges of history. The self-seeking and self-important inevitably become petty and insignificant.

True greatness only comes when a person concentrates his love and attention on something beyond himself. For Moses it was freeing men from slavery so that they could be released for true worship. For Socrates it was understanding. For Michelangelo it was painting which gave expression to truth. For Tolstoy it was literature that gave expression to truth. For Einstein it was Science that explained the "Reason that manifests itself in nature." For Jesus it was the redemption of men from their failures and delusions so they could again know God and attain the stature and majesty for which He had created them. Everyone who has had a positive impact on human history has given more importance to the Purpose or Product than to personal fulfillment. That single focus upon something beyond ourselves, something that is greater than ourselves, has the power to turn even the mundane into a powerful vehicle of human advancement.

Whatever is worth doing is worth doing well. Whatever is worth our top priority is worth doing with all of our hearts. When our concentration becomes focused upon the Product or Purpose, power is released. It is easy for leaders to become like flood lamps spreading their interests in too many directions. If they would concentrate on just doing one thing well their life force would become focused like a laser with great power being released. When George Washington Carver focused on the lowly peanut the entire world benefitted. The apostle Paul said "This *one* thing I do," and the mere letters penned by this man of focused vision have impacted the world more than the writings of almost all others combined; after nearly two thousand years they still help to chart the course of the world.

Greatness does not result from wanting to be great, but by the determination to take something outside of ourselves to greater heights. Regardless of who we are, and what level of human esteem and position we now hold, if we will identify our Purpose or Product and make it the focus of our attention and effort, we will make a difference.

As Martin Luther King, Jr. understood, the best street sweeper can be more important than the corporate executive or government official who lives by lesser standards. Like Moses who delivered men from taskmasters, you can transform the task into the vehicle to freedom through the fulfillment of Purpose. Men can take an important job and do it with mediocrity and be considered significant while they are in fact failures. The one who takes a mediocre task and raises it to the level of significance is an artist who deserves the world's attention; he is truly a great leader.

THE PRACTICAL PRINCIPLES OF THE PRODUCT

The first step toward making your Product successful is to make it your passion. If you are not in love with your Product it may be hard for anyone else to even like it. The passion of true love is more contagious than any disease. If you are passionate about your Product that passion will spread to others. Victor Kiam loved the Remington razor enough to buy the whole company. His entire sales pitch was his passion for that razor and that passion sold more razors than price or quality had ever been able to sell.

The next principle is to make your product at least useful, but if possible, to make it essential. There must be a Purpose for the Product. George Washington Carver took the peanut, which was on or near the bottom of just about everyone's priority list, and made it useful, even essential, in some of its discovered applications. George Washington Carver's life is a testimony that, regardless of how insignificant we feel that our Product or Service is, if we are devoted enough we can discover applications that will raise its value and usefulness. Creativity must be applied in making the Product *and* in finding applications for its use.

The next principle for making your Product successful is to price it fairly. The more fair the price the more successful you will ultimately be. Pricing should be determined by what we *should* get, not what we *could* get. If you take advantage of a present monopoly or critical need for your Product to squeeze all that you can out of those who need it, you may get their present business, but you will not get their future business if they can possibly give it to anyone else. Greed kills when it comes to enterprise. *You can shear a sheep many times but you can only skin it once.*

If you are now thinking that this is all idealistic you are right, to a degree. Idealism can be a delusion that can lead to extinction, but a lack of idealism *will* lead to extinction. If you have abandoned all idealism for the sake of gain you have lost your humanity and any potential for significance.

Unfortunately, "the ugly American" is a title earned by many U.S. businessmen and officials abroad. Not only have we been arrogant and presumptuous, we have tried to compensate for lack of quality and value in our Product by using hype and manipulation. That may work for a little while, but it will always result in ultimate failure.

Just a few decades ago Americans were esteemed as honest and straightforward individuals who would do business with a handshake. Then a subtle form of legalism crept into the fiber of the nation and whatever was *legal* was considered to be right. "If you can get away with it you should do it" became a basic philosophy. If a future historian writes about the Rise and Fall of America he will almost certainly discover this subtle but terrible deception to be the ax that felled this great and mighty tree. If we do not make dramatic and substantial changes, "Made in America" will soon become an epithet for poor quality, overpricing and dependence upon hype in place of integrity. If you are motivated to do what you can get away with, you are an enemy of humanity. Like Judas, you may have gained your silver but you have lost your soul.

We must return to the ideals of honesty, and value, and we must ponder the Purpose for which we are offering our Product. The world really does want to love and respect the American, but it is up to us to give them a reason to.

Chapter Ten

Administration Part I

The Administration is the brain and nervous system of every enterprise; through it all of the other Essentials are controlled just like all of the organs in our body are controlled by our brain. Regardless of the quality and strength of the other Essentials, if your administration is not functioning properly, your venture will be like a healthy body with a sick mind—caught somewhere between out of control and completely useless. Likewise, if your Administration is healthy it may be able to compensate for even serious problems in the other essential areas.

CONTROL GROWTH OR FIGHT CANCER

Administration is where all enterprises begin. No one has ever started a venture until someone made the decision to do it, and decisions are the function of Administration. After this initial decision to start, most of the attention then usually goes to the Product, Marketing, Resources and Timing. The Administration of many ventures just evolves, coming together piecemeal, born more out of necessity and crisis than quality planning. This is another major cause of failure in enterprise.

Left to form by circumstances without planning, Administration will become a cancer with its greatest devotion being the feeding of itself. It will keep growing until it has sapped the life out of the rest of the enterprise. Management has a way of increasing layer by layer until it is inefficient and ineffective, becoming more of a burden than the life force it must be for true success.

Many governments are good examples of Administrations which have gone awry. In 1980 the U.S. welfare departments had more than one employee for each recipient of benefits! If the welfare of the less fortunate were the priority, this preposterous ratio would never have been allowed. Obviously the promotion of the department became more important than the reason for which it was created.

The Administrations of many corporations are just as unhealthy. So are those of many schools, hospitals, charities, churches or ministries. Because Administration is the brain and nervous system of the enterprise, if cancer begins to grow here it will be most deadly.

How is this to be avoided? The development and control of our Administration must be given at least as much attention and planning as the other Essentials. This can only be provided by effective, discerning leadership.

THE OVERLOAD: FRIEND OR ENEMY?

An effective leader must be positive in his orientation, but he must know how to say a most important word: **"No!"** For example: If an administration is being dictated by crisis management instead of sound planning, it will want to hire more people every time the work load becomes heavy. Our first response to an overload should not be to throw more money or resources at it, but to use the pressure as an opportunity to find better and more efficient ways to do the job. An efficiently managed enterprise *will be overloaded* part of the time.

There are cycles to almost all activity. If you are overloaded one third of the time you will likely be under loaded at least that much. The leader must navigate a tolerable median between the overload and the underload for maximum efficiency. Overloads can be creative pressures we need to help us improve our systems and strengthen the muscles of our enterprise. Just throwing more Resources at the overloads will only increase the fat, which will weaken the heart of the venture.

President Jimmy Carter once proposed a "zero based budget." Under this plan every department in government would start with a budget of zero at the beginning of each new fiscal year and would then have to justify every dollar it was given. If the leadership to actually implement this program had existed, it would have greatly increased efficiency in the Federal Government, and may well have cut the federal deficit to "zero." Some safeguards would have been required, but something of this nature must be instituted before the weight of our government destroys the supporting economy.

If there is no system for effectively making Administration accountable on a regular basis it will become fat or cancerous. Left to itself, Administration will quickly begin to think and act as though the entire enterprise exists for its benefit instead of the other way around. It takes constant vigilance on the part of leadership to keep this from happening.

THE REWARD FACTOR

In management *you will get what you reward*, not what you want to get, or even what you plan to get. Many ventures and enterprises, even though their emphasis, training and effort is devoted to efficient management, fail to ever achieve it because they actually reward mediocrity and penalize efficiency. If there is no accountability the most inefficient departments will end up with the most people, the biggest budgets, the most prestige, power and influence. At the same time, the most efficient department which has kept its staff lean and effective, will actually lose influence and reward. If you want an efficient Administration you must reward efficiency, and penalize inefficiency and waste.

THE CHIEF EXECUTIVE OFFICER

For simplicity we are using the title C.E.O. as the head of the enterprise. The title used in your organization may be anything from general to pastor.

The C.E.O. should be a leader, rather than a manager type. He gives direction to the enterprise. He must be the one with the vision of where it's going and which goals are to be pursued. The best C.E.O. will be concept oriented, able to grasp the overall picture. However, he must also be able to understand the details or he will be inclined to give unrealistic goals and poor direction, causing confusion instead of inspiration.

The C.E.O. is a lonely position. The opportunities are great but so are the difficulties. He is often the only one who can see the big picture. The managers responsible for the other Essentials will usually feel that their departments are the most important in the company, and, to a degree, they should feel that way. The C.E.O. must encourage the loyalty of each department head to his department, but also be able to balance the pressure he gets from each in order to stay on course. To do this the C.E.O. must know where he's going and have the courage and fortitude to disregard pressures when necessary, or take other proper actions.

TENACITY TEMPERED BY FLEXIBILITY

The C.E.O., like the captain of a ship, must know his destination and the course for getting there, before he leaves port. Almost every plan will still require some changes, because every voyage has surprises which are not in the plan. The captain must be able to adjust for these surprises while staying as close as possible to the intended course. It is easy to lay out the course while you're in port, but it can be far more difficult to recompute your navigation after storms have blown you far from your planned position.

As the captain you must make the decision when not to let the storm blow you off course. When a person first looks down on a river from an airplane he is usually surprised by the way they snake through the countryside, curling and weaving, usually traveling several times the distance from beginning to end than if they had just gone straight. Why do rivers flow like that? Because they take the path of least resistance. If you are inclined to allow resistance to change your course, you are going to be traveling many times the necessary distance to get to your intended goal. Most vessels do not have the fuel or resources to go very far from the original plan. Your judgment in this alone may be the difference between success and failure.

As an aircraft pilot, I determined that it was in my best interest to become the best one possible. I asked for the toughest and most intimidating instructors, and then I would antagonize them into becoming even meaner. I knew that if I could not operate an aircraft properly under their pressure there could be emergency situations that I would have trouble coping with. There were days when I would get back from a training flight and never want to see an airplane again. It was humiliating and frustrating, but later when I got into some of the storms that were to take me to the very limits of my skills, I thanked the Lord many times for the toughness of those instructors.

Arrogance causes us to become unteachable whereas humility keeps us continually learning. **Training** and **Preparation** never end for the great leaders and managers. Preparation and planning will help you to make the *best* choices in whatever circumstances you find yourself.

TWO KINDS OF LEADERSHIP

There are two basic approaches to leadership, the aggressive and the conservative, though there may be unlimited variations of each. There are advantages to each of these approaches. With few exceptions the most renowned leaders in history have been of the extreme aggressive nature. However, the overwhelming majority of successful leaders, though maybe less notable, have been the conservative type. The aggressive leaders who can adjust and be conservative when it is appropriate are the most successful of all. Few have achieved this flexibility. Let's briefly look at each type of leader.

THE AGGRESSOR

These are the home run hitters. They almost hate singles and want to swing for the fences every time they come to the plate. Like a home run, their successes are spectacular; but if you swing for the fences you are going to strike out more often. The same attitude that leads to the greatest successes also leads to the most devastating failures. If we are afraid to fail we will never succeed, because we will never really play the game.

The greatest leaders have learned to use their failures as opportunities for reaching even greater heights. We usually learn more from failure than we do from success. Those who attain a degree of success without failure will tend to be superficial and naive. These are easily spotted as the ones who have all the answers. The truly great leaders will be those who would rather listen than talk, always seeking more understanding. Consider this about Abraham Lincoln, one of the greatest leaders ever produced by America:

1831   He failed in business

1832   He was defeated for the Legislature

1833   He failed again in business

1836   He suffered a nervous breakdown

1838   He was defeated for Speaker of the Legislature

1840   He was defeated for Elector

1843   He was defeated for Congress

1848   He was defeated again for Congress

1855   He was defeated for the Senate

1856   He was defeated for Vice President

1858   He was defeated for the Senate again

1860   He was elected President

He preserved the Union

It is hard to comprehend how a man could endure the continual crises and pressures Abraham Lincoln suffered while president. The list above explains such endurance. The man was well acquainted with failure—but he was never a quitter! Every defeat made Lincoln more determined and more prepared for his ultimate task. Setbacks will either make us *better* or they will make us *bitter*; the choice is up to us.

We will learn far more from our failures than from our victories, but we must never become satisfied with failure. When we resign ourselves to failure we become a failure. But if we will use our failures to increase our ultimate resolve, we are destined for victory.

The aggressive category of leader has produced the most renowned and memorable characters in history. Brilliant victories and devastating failures punctuate each of their lives. Austerlitz then Waterloo, Chancelorsville then Gettysburg.

They win big and lose big, but they play the game with all of their heart.

Those with this nature would rather lose it all than live any other way. If you are not of this nature it is almost impossible to understand those who are. They are few in number but the course of history has followed in their wake. If you are one of these, or if you work for one, you're in for a wild ride. They live perpetually on the thin line between heartbreaking disaster and breathtaking achievement.

The following are some of the Characteristics of the Aggressor Temperament:

THE AGGRESSOR	
Strengths	**Weaknesses**
Seldom discouraged	Lacks compassion, hard
Will take charge without hesitation	Impatient
Decisive	Sets standards too high, expects too much from others
Adventurous	Seldom gives praise to others
Will not quit	Impetuous, makes rash decisions
	Will not retreat even when it is strategic and wise
	Overcommits

THE CONSERVATIVE

The Conservative leaders are no less important to progress and success. Without them the chaos would probably be unbearable. They provide stability and longevity. Their lives may be unspectacular, but are usually meaningful and fulfilling. These are not the salt of the earth—they *are* the earth, and they tend to move about as fast as the earth changes. Nevertheless, their genius can be profound.

General Longstreet, a division commander in Lee's Army of Northern Virginia, was of this nature. In many of the successful battles he may have been as responsible for victory as the more famous Stonewall Jackson. He did not move as fast, but neither was he moved from his position quickly. Many historians believe that Longstreet deserved the nickname "Stonewall" more than Jackson, if you look at the whole course of the war. He was unspectacular but consistent. On one hand, his slow movement at Gettysburg may have cost the Confederacy a sweeping victory and the war. Even so, had Lee listened to his counsel there would not have been a "Pickett's charge," which did cost them the battle and probably the war.

When the conservative leader loses it is usually because he fails to take advantage of opportunity. He wins sometimes simply because he is the only one left. If an enterprise can have a partnership of leaders with each of these natures, as the Army of Northern Virginia did while Jackson was alive, it can have the greatest opportunity of all.

After Gettysburg Lee paid more attention to Longstreet. If you consider the increased odds they were facing, they won some of their most remarkable battles during this time. Some historians claim they never really lost another battle—they just ran out of men and resources. You can see Longstreet's defensive genius in all of these conflicts. The tactics he devised were actually those most used by armies around the world for the next one hundred years. Even so, history does not remember Longstreet as well as it does Lee and Jackson. Seldom will men, or history, give this type of solid leader their due, but they are no less responsible for shaping history or present human affairs.

True wisdom in leadership is to know when to be aggressive and when to be conservative. This can be determined by the status of the Essentials in your enterprise.

I owned one business which was much like Lee's army: I was so short of resources that I had no choice but to be aggressive—it was my only long term hope for survival. When I came to my Gettysburg, the chance for total victory, I too had a "Longstreet"—my comptroller. He begged me to be conservative, but I had won so many victories against great odds I had begun to think that I could not lose. This is the Titanic syndrome, and it may not be curable until you've had at least one good ship sink from under you. Victories can make you feel so invincible that you sail recklessly into the most treacherous of waters.

On the other hand, you may never truly know how to win until you've failed. The wisest and most effective leaders have usually tasted many devastating defeats. An amazing number of America's most successful business leaders have been through at least one bankruptcy. Unfortunately for American business, we tend to shoot our own wounded so that some of those who could be the very best leaders never get a second chance. Those who have never tasted losing may be the most dangerous of all. Remember Captain Edward J. Smith; he had never made a maritime mistake. Because of that he was chosen to skipper the Titanic on her maiden voyage. *There is great danger in being overly conservative.*

THE OPPORTUNITY OF ADVERSITY

Almost anyone can lead when things are going well; it is the ability to handle crisis that separates the true leaders from the pretenders. To most, crises are the threat of disaster, but to true leaders they are opportunities—they thrive on the intensity of the moment. But you cannot do this with a clarity of mind if you are gripped with the fear of failure.

Many Southerners still like to talk about how they would have won the war had Lee not tried to invade the North. It does not take a military genius to realize this as a fallacy. Crisis is defined as the point at which it is determined if a patient is going to live or die. The Confederacy had reached precisely that point. Vicksburg was about to fall and the Confederacy would be cut in half. Resources were running dangerously low and the fighting and foraging of the two armies had destroyed the crops in most of Virginia for two years. With all of the great victories accomplished by the Confederate Army, the South was still on the verge of collapse. Conventional wisdom said they should withdraw to a few states which they could hold. In one of the boldest and greatest decisions in military history, Lee decided it was time to attack. When it looked as if all was lost he brought the Confederacy to the very threshold of total victory.

The whole world was amazed by Lee's boldness; several major nations were ready to recognize the Confederacy and come to their aid had he won just one battle on Union soil. Even with the heart breaking defeat at Gettysburg, Lee probably gave the Confederacy an extra year of existence. Not only had the Virginia farmers been given a badly needed growing season, the Army of Northern Virginia brought back several month's worth of supplies from their foraging in the North. Sometimes a good offense is the best defense, but the timid seldom see this opportunity. The greatest crisis can be our biggest opportunity if we can stay cool enough to take advantage of it.

THE DANGER OF PROSPERITY

Just as a crisis can be an opportunity for victory, prevailing prosperity can lead to defeat. Who can count the great sports teams which have fallen to weak competitors while riding extended winning streaks? History is littered with empires which received their fatal wounds while at the height of their achievement. Success can make you vulnerable to a devastating blow when you least expect it.

If you are one of the few who cannot be satisfied until you stand at the pinnacle, you *must* go for it. You will be a drag on society and a pain to everyone around you until you do. But listen to the conservatives when they speak, and be ready to heed their advice when it is appropriate. Not only can they help you get to the top, they can help you stay there.

If you're willing to live with small victories you will probably only have to absorb small defeats. If this is more in line with your nature, do not try to be something else, or you'll perish from ulcers and heart attacks. Even so, pay attention to those who are of the aggressive nature. They may open your eyes to opportunities which can be attained even within your comfortable level of risk. They may also help you to see when you have no choice but to risk it all; and those choices sometimes come even to the most conservative players.

The following are some of the general characteristics of those with the conservative temperament:

THE CONSERVATIVE	
Strengths	**Weaknesses**
Plans well	Misses opportunity
Is good under pressure, seldom overreacts	Tends to major on minors
Faithful to commitments	Boring to others
Thoughtful	Will retreat too quickly
Accomplishes goals	
Is seldom surprised by circumstances	
Patient	

THE EFFECTIVE MIDDLE MANAGER

This is usually the toughest position in any organization. Here you get most of the blame and very little of the credit. Middle management is an awkward, inhospitable position for any person, so do not expect to feel comfortable here. No one aspires to being a middle manager as their ultimate goal; it is a stepping stone to greater things. However, most who make it to this position, remain there. The overwhelming majority of those who have come here die in this wilderness and never make it to their promised land.

When Moses led the Israelites out of Egypt with visions of their promised land, the entire first generation died in the wilderness without ever seeing that land. They died in that wilderness for the same reason most die in the wilderness of middle management—they stopped believing and started complaining. Complaining darkens the soul. Complaining does not build up, it tears down, and only builders go beyond the level of middle management.

Moses told Israel that they had been led into the wilderness for testing and to humble them. Middle management is meant to accomplish the same purpose. Everyone does well when everything is going right. Who will maintain composure and steadfastness in the midst of difficulties and apparent unfairness? Only the ones who have the real thing. Everyone *wants* to get to the top. Only one in a thousand wants to bad enough to pay the price. The wilderness of middle management separates the pretenders to the throne from the truly anointed.

While Israel was in Egypt they were promised a land flowing with milk and honey. In the place to which they were first taken there was not even any water! It was the exact opposite of what they had been promised! Middle management will usually be the exact opposite of everything that you had envisioned for your career. The cold slap in the face usually comes quickly after entering this position. Here there is pressure without relief, sacrifice without reward. It will make you bitter or it will make you better, but it *will* make you different. Here you will increase your resolve, or you will lose your reward. Here, without determination and discipline, your vision will vanish into daydreams that will never become realities.

The Lord really did have a promised land for Israel, and He did not want the first generation to perish in the wilderness. If you have made it to middle management you are on the course to fulfill your goals and you really can get there.

THE TEST OF FAITH

As stated, it will require faith to enter your promised land. Faith is defined by *Funk & Wagnals Standard Handbook of Synonyms, Antonyms & Prepositions* as "a union of belief and trust; it is a belief so strong that it becomes a part of one's own nature."

Faith is stronger than belief. To believe is to give intellectual assent; to have faith is to be inseparable from the object of your devotion. Belief can be changed or lost by a more persuasive argument; true faith is so much a part of the person it can only be taken by death.

Faith is usually understood in religious terms but we must understand—*everyone has religion.* Faith is the substance of our very existence and identity; our faith is who we are. All have faith; it is what we have our faith in that determines which religion it is. (Even atheism is actually a religion under the basic faith of "humanism.") The stronger the faith one has, the stronger his existence and the more impact he will have. The more positive the faith the more constructive this impact will be.

Faith can also have a "dark side." It was Hitler's faith in his demented racism that drove him to extraordinary accomplishments that will scar humanity for generations. We must ask: What is our faith in? Is it a positive or negative faith? How strong is it?

In Christianity this difference between "belief" and "faith" is the difference between being a truly devoted follower of Christ and a mere pretender who has deluded himself in order to appease his conscience. That is why the great genius of Christianity, the apostle Paul, stated that it was the faith that is of the *heart,* not just the mind, that resulted in salvation. The popular and pervasive "believing in God," that is just believing that He exists, accomplishes little and is not the true Christian "faith." The delusion that we just need to believe in His existence hinders the pilgrim from finding the true religion of *faith in God.*

The same principle is true in every aspect of life and enterprise. There is a wide gulf between believing in one's goals and having faith in them. That gulf separates those who succeed from those who spend their lives wandering aimlessly in the wilderness; these may cover a lot of ground but they are going in circles and not really getting anywhere.

A person without faith is like a car without an engine; it may have a beautiful appearance but it will not get you anywhere. The stronger the faith, the further and the faster you will go. Mere belief is superficial and accomplishes little more than appeasing the emotions. Faith is a living power that can move the mountains that stand in the way of its accomplishment.

Moses led Israel into the wilderness in order to change their superstitions and limited belief into a rock solid faith. Your wilderness, whether it is the mire of middle management, or other circumstances that have you in a place which is the opposite of where you intended to go, can accomplish the same for you. If you respond properly to your wilderness it will turn emotional frivolity into a force! Embrace your difficulties as opportunities and you *will* get to your promised land. Let the difficulties discourage you and you too will perish in that place and never accomplish your goals.

THE TEST OF FREEDOM

Moses could lead Israel out of Egypt, but he could not take the Egypt out of the Israelites—the difficulties of the wilderness were meant to do that. The Israelites had been slaves in Egypt; slavery is the most base human condition but there is a security in slavery that is hard to get free of. Even though the Israelites were freed and moving toward their destiny and fulfillment, when they encountered difficulties most of them began looking back on the terrible oppression of slavery wanting to go back, feeling that they had been better off in Egypt!

This is the dividing line that separates those who go on to victory from those who go back to their doom—no one will attain his goal or destiny until he becomes *free*. The free man would rather perish in the wilderness trying than to go back to slavery. Until we make the decision that we will not go back, regardless of how bad it gets, we will not go forward.

The most telltale symptom of surrender to slavery is **grumbling** and **complaining.** The one who complains has lost the faith; he has already given up in his heart. The one with true faith meets even the biggest obstacles as an opportunity to win a bigger victory, and make a greater advance toward his goal. This cannot be blind optimism, which is just another form of mere belief masquerading as the true faith. Optimism will wither in the heat of the desert wilderness; true faith becomes stronger and more determined as the heat is turned up.

Faith can move mountains and it will move every one that stands in its way. True faith makes the road; it does not follow one. That is why true faith is true freedom; *no* shackle can be put on it. True faith is the ability to seize the vision of one's destiny with such a grip that it cannot be taken away until it is fulfilled. True faith moves every obstacle, but is moved by no obstacle. True faith *will* get to the promised land.

The first three days that the Israelites were in the wilderness, they did not even have water. Then the first well that they were taken to was bitter! This was unquestionably a trial. They did not understand that God intended to turn the bitter waters into sweet as an object lesson. Their first response to the disappointment was doubt and complaining, and by that the destroyer was released among them.

Anyone who has been truly thirsty can identify with the Israelites. Real thirst arouses our basic instincts of survival. They may have had a real excuse to complain but this most difficult test was also their greatest opportunity. It is the real test that brings out real faith. True faith is internal, not external and it is not dependent on external circumstances. **True faith does not change with disappointments; it becomes even stronger. True faith will always turn the bitter waters of disappointment into the sweet waters of greater opportunity.** When disappointment results in complaining, the destroyer of our faith has been released and our vision will soon perish.

The wilderness, whether it be middle management, the middle class, or middle-age, is meant to bring out the best, or the worst, in you. You are the one who determines the outcome.

Chapter Eleven

Administration Part II

THE SUCCESSFUL NON-MANAGER

The non-manager will have one of two goals: either to become a manager or not to become one. Success is not determined by how far one advances up the management ladder, but by how well he accomplishes his *own* goals. One may not want to advance in management for reasons more noble than those of the one who wants to go to the top. For example: management may require too much time and attention which could otherwise be spent with family, church, civic or charitable organizations. Not everyone's primary goal in life will be job related. There are many perfectly valid reasons for avoiding management. Those who do not have ambitions of advancing in position can be just as valuable, important and successful as anyone else in the enterprise.

How many battles which set the course of history have been turned by a single individual in the lines who determined that he would not run, which gave courage to a few more, who gave courage to a few more, until the lines held, the battle was turned, and the outcome of history was changed. Journalists and historians give the credit for such victories to the generals, but mere privates who took their stand and refused to retreat have probably won just as many of those battles, their courage sometimes overcoming the incompetent tactics of their generals. This is not to detract from the many great and competent generals of history, but good men have sometimes made a foolish strategy look brilliant. The best leadership can emerge from any level. The best leadership is to have the wisdom and will to implement that which needs to be done for success.

OUR GREATEST ASSET

General Patton, one of the most effective generals of World War II, placed the training of his men as his number one priority. He pushed them beyond the standards of the rest of the army. He then won victory after victory with strategies no one else thought would work, and they probably would not have worked with anyone else's men. The exceptional training and conditioning of his men gave him options not available to others.

Whatever the enterprise, your people are your strongest asset. Few companies have become so automated that its people do not still radically affect its success or failure. A sports team may have stars on its roster, but the skill and devotion to the rest of the team will be just as essential to the team's success. A church may have a great preacher, but it will be the commitment of its members that determines whether it will produce lasting fruit. Like Patton, if you make your people your top priority and highest interest, you will be able to press beyond the present limits of performance.

As we have already determined, leadership and management are not the same thing. You can be a great leader without even being in a management position. How many workers in a factory have affected the success of the entire company by taking their stand against bitterness, resentment, gossip, and slander. Those in the lowest positions can have the strength of character that will be an irresistible example setting the thermostat of morale throughout the company. Those leaders need to be trained, recognized and rewarded as much as an effective manager, because they are doing just as much for you.

THE FIRST STEP IN MAKING LEADERS

You can train someone to be a manager but leadership skills must be imparted by example. The first step in imparting leadership is to communicate a respect for others. By the very definition of *leader*, he cannot be one who pushes his people forward; he must be the one who *leads* them—from the front. No one will follow a person they do not respect. Respect is a foundation for leadership.

Again, an incontrovertible law of nature is that we reap what we sow. If we sow bitterness it will come back to us. If we sow strife it will return to us. If we sow respect there will be a harvest of the same. If we sow respect in our people they will respect us, each other, and themselves.

With respect we will see leadership begin to sprout in those whom we least expect it. It was just hidden under the lack of self-esteem that respect helped them to overcome. With self-respect comes courage which *always* results in people rising above their previous level of performance. Of the privates who took their stands and turned battles, not one of them did it without planting his feet in respect for his country, his cause, his unit, his family and himself. True leadership has a strong foundation and purpose from which it cannot be separated. Respect is the cement of that foundation.

TIME MANAGEMENT

Managing your time properly is essential to being both an effective leader and manager. One workable time management plan is to designate one day for each of the Five Essentials of your enterprise. Figure 1 shows a sample schedule for a corporate leader.

Monday — Administration

1) Review and plan your schedule.
2) Evaluate general goals and progress toward their accomplishment, necessary corrections and changes.
3) Evaluate the effectiveness and progress toward the goals of each of the other Five Essentials
4) Study Administration and evaluate the efficiency and effectiveness of this department.
5) Meet with the Administration manager.
6) Plan. (Your planning will always be more effective if you designate specific time just for it.)
7) Review employee relations, benefits, etc.

Tuesday — The Product

1) Evaluate your Product.
2) Evaluate the Products of your competitors, new innovations, etc.
3) Meet with the Product Development manager.

Wednesday — Marketing

1) Evaluate sales.
2) Evaluate marketing strategy and advertising.
3) Evaluate sales staff.
4) Meet with Marketing Manager.
5) Study Marketing, trade magazines, etc.

Thursday — Resources

1) Review accounting reports such as P&L, Balance Sheet, Cash Flow projections, etc.
2) Study capitalization and know options for accomplishing goals, plan for greater efficiency and/or flexibility, etc.
3) Meet with accountants, communicate with bankers, brokers, etc.
4) Study capitalization or other resources relevant to your enterprise.

Friday — Timing

1) Evaluate trends in products, markets, financing, etc.
2) Return phone calls. (NOTE: The phone is one of the most powerful tools of any business, but it can also be the most disruptive. If you will designate a specific time for returning all but the most crucial phone calls, it can radically improve your productivity all week).
3) Devote a period of time for making up unfininshed business from Monday through Thursday.

Figure 1 – Sample Schedule for a Corporate Leader

Being able to make *and keep* a schedule is fundamental to efficient management of our time, which is a most valuable asset. Every schedule requires some flexibility, but seldom as much as we tend to give it. The average manager wastes more than 30% of his time sporadically going from one task to another and then back again.

We must learn to only let emergencies or matters of extreme and defined importance distract us from our schedules. If something about Marketing comes in on Monday put it in the Wednesday basket and do not even look at it until Wednesday. If our bank statement comes in on Tuesday put it in the Thursday basket and do not look at it until Thursday. You will be amazed at how much more you can accomplish with such a schedule and how much less stress you will have with such a simple routine.

Undefined goals and undefined priorities are two of the biggest factors which sap efficiency and productivity. *Lists and checklists* can be simple but effective remedies to these problems. Making purposeful lists and checklists is an "art," a skill to be developed and perfected. If used properly, this skill has the ability to radically impact the efficiency of almost anyone. Like any other "art," there are basics to be learned that apply to almost everyone, but after that you must develop your own style. A few of the basics for developing lists would include:

1) **Start with a "Things To Do List."** This type of list works as a reminder and an organizer. Just seeing what you put in writing will help you to keep your time and efforts on course and reduce distractions.

2) **Build your lists around goals.** The purpose of the list is to help you organize in order to accomplish your goals. List your goals and then what will be required to accomplish each one

under it. Leave space for adding to the list things
that are brought to your attention or memory.

3) **Prioritize your lists.** A simple priority scale of
1 to 5 works well. Do not work on the 3's until
the 1's and 2's have been completed.

Keep a note pad with you at all times, and use it! Whenever
you are told to do something or you see something that needs
to be done, or when you get a new idea, write it down. You
will be amazed at how your personal efficiency can actually
be increased by simply developing this art of making lists.

Developing and using simple, brief **checklists** can also
dramatically impact the efficiency of the average enterprise.
Like lists, keeping checklists simple and usable is the key to
their effectiveness. As an example, Figure 2 shows a checklist
devised for getting a newsletter ready for mailing.

You may also benefit from keeping your completed checklists for future reference. They can help you determine that
one or more of the tasks will take more time than allotted, etc.

Another valuable tool for efficient management is the "art"
of filing. Most filing systems are designed for storing things
instead of retrieving them. An inefficient filing system can
cost the average enterprise a veritable fortune over just a few
years. The time spent designing an efficient system can pay
great dividends in future productivity.

SUMMARY

Like the brain and the nervous system, Administration
must have a working partnership between Leadership and
Management. The brain gives the signals but the nervous
system must carry the signal to the proper organ or limb to
initiate the action. It is imperative that Leadership and Management realize that they are different from one another, that
they see from different perspectives and have different priorities. These differences are complimentary and not conflicting.

Factors: Mail Date: July 1
Printer needs 2 weeks
3 days required for sorting

1 ☐ Articles completed
Needed by June 1
Completed _____

2 ☐ Layout completed
Needed by June 7
Completed _____

3 ☐ Inserts designed
Needed by June 7
Completed _____

4 ☐ Deliver layout to printer
Needed by June 10
Completed _____

5 ☐ Envelopes ordered
Needed by June 10
Completed _____

6 ☐ Purge mailing list
Needed by June 20
Completed _____

7 ☐ Print labels
Needed by June 23
Completed _____

8 ☐ Pick up from printer
Needed by June 24
Completed _____

9 ☐ Label & Sort for mailing
Needed by June 30
Completed _____

Figure 2 – Sample Checklist for a Newsletter Mailing

For effective Administration there must be a unity of purpose and communication established between the Leaders and the Managers, with each learning from and adapting some of the characteristics of the other.

I have purposely emphasized the differences between Leadership and Management because they are seldom understood, but every leader will have to do some managing and almost every manager will have to lead. It is true that the more these two can specialize in their own fields the more effective they will usually be.

But what about those enterprises that are too small to allow for a distinction—like the small shop where the owner is the leader and manager? If you are in a place where you have to be both leader and manager, there can still be a separation between your duties that will enable you to be more effective at both. You can devote your Mondays to strategy and planning (leadership) and another day(s) to implementation (management). If you will discipline yourself to not be distracted from planning during the time you have devoted to it you will be amazed at how much more clear your direction will become. Then, when you give yourself to managing and implementing your plans you will be amazed at how much more effective you can be. It is the proper blending of these areas that leads to successful Administration.

Chapter Twelve

Marketing

You can have the best Product, Administration, Timing and be well Capitalized, but weak **Marketing** can be your downfall. Regardless of how much you love the Product, how well it is made or how great a value it is, if it is not effectively marketed it will be difficult to succeed. Some of the world's best Products, offered at exceptional values, have failed because of weak Marketing.

In this study we define Marketing as both *Promotions* and *Distribution* because they are essentially linked. This chapter is not meant to be a comprehensive study of Marketing, but an overview of some general principles that true and lasting success depend upon.

STRATEGIC RESEARCH

Effective Marketing must begin with a thorough knowledge of your market. Only then will you be able to develop a strategy for best reaching it. If you do not have this knowledge, you must then develop a plan for researching it.

Often market research will be as important as the research you did developing the Product. At least part of this research should be done before developing the Product. You can have the greatest widget in the world but if only three people in the world need one, and two already have them, you have a slim chance for success. The bigger the market for your Product the greater the prospects for your success. The smaller or more competitive the market, the more skilled you will have to be in promoting it.

Time and resources wisely spent researching your market can save you many times what you spend. Not only can this research help to identify your market, but it may help develop the Product, determine the quality, quantity and price of what you produce, and to give you a head start for distributing the Product when it is ready. As stated, some of this research should be done before you begin development and production, and on a regular basis afterwards, because markets are continually changing.

There are many fine marketing research firms that can probably do this study for you much more accurately and less expensively than you can do it yourself. These independent studies can also be a big help in raising needed capital for your enterprise. Every banker and investor knows that as unbiased as you may try to be in your own study, your love for the Product, or dreams of success will affect your results. A good marketing research firm is going to find out and tell you the truth, and you must know the truth about your market in order to succeed.

HITTING THE TARGET

Many a great and potentially successful Product failed to succeed simply because the Promotions targeted the *wrong market*. Had these targeted the right market with their efforts they would have probably succeeded.

Let us use this book for example. With a few exceptions, only scholars and educators are naturally attracted to thick, hardbound books. Also, after a book reaches 150 pages in length it will lose approximately one percent of its potential readers for every two pages added. Therefore a book of 250 pages will have lost about fifty percent of the potential readers of a 150 page book.

Those who like thin books are on both ends of the social strata; busy corporate executives and high achievers like them because they take less time; others like them because they are less intimidating. On the other hand, scholars and educators, who like thick, hardbound books, usually view thinner books as having less substance, and therefore less worthy of their attention.

If your book is targeting busy corporate executives but is 350 pages in length, you will probably only reach a small percentage of those you would have attracted with a more compact volume. There are authors who target scholars with their content, but who produce the smaller, paperback books they tend to resist. Others, who produce the large, hardbound volumes which scholars are attracted to, write them in a personal, popular style that most scholars do not appreciate. Those who might appreciate the style of writing do not like the size of the book! The audience a writer is trying to reach should be considered while the book is being planned.

Each chapter of this book could easily have been expanded into a complete volume of 150 pages or more, or combined into one large volume of almost 1,000 pages, but the achievers and entrepreneurs I wanted to reach would not have read it. I determined to lay out the basic principles in this one compact book; if it proves successful I may consider publishing more advanced studies in subsequent volumes of about the same length. On the other hand, if I were targeting scholars and educators I would have gone with the thicker, hardbound version.

A visit to a quality advertising agency, or business research firm can not only save a great deal of time and resources, it could even save you from failure. The average producer does not think like the average consumer. *You probably do not think like your customers, or potential customers.* Effective research can help you to understand their perspective so that your Product more perfectly meets their needs or desires, which may or may not be yours.

The following are some questions you may need to answer in order to develop an effective Marketing strategy:

- Who *needs* your product?
- How can you most effectively communicate and educate them about your Product?
- Should you go directly to the potential customers or through a wholesaler(s) or other middlemen?
- If you go through a wholesaler, who should take care of the promotions, or what portion of them?
- Are there trade publications which effectively reach your target customer?
- What will be the best timing for your advertising?
- Is your Product more suited to a short term, high profile Promotion strategy, or a more long term consistent strategy?
- What other forms of advertising would be effective for your Product?
- Do you need your own sales force, or can you use independents?
- What will motivate them to give top priority to promoting your Product?
- Has there been a recent polling of your target customer base that has information you can use, or should you consider having this done?
- Who are your competitors? What are their strengths and weaknesses? How loyal are their customers? How can you use their advertising to your benefit?

- Can you qualify your promotions for free radio or T.V. public service announcements?

- What potential customers may not *need* your Product, but could *use* it? For example: If your product is bottled mineral water, cities with poorly rated or bad tasting water may *need* your product, while others may not be quite so desperate for it, but it would still be better for them.

These are just a few standard questions you will need to answer in order to effectively promote your Product. There may be others that relate to you and your Product specifically. Factors such as size of the enterprise, market, the cost of developing the Product, can determine how comprehensive this research needs to be.

THE ONE FOR ALL AND ALL FOR ONE TRAP

Many enterprises get started and succeed on the strength of just one customer, but these are usually living on the edge of disaster. The more diversified your customer base, the more secure your enterprise will be. Even with the best intentions on the part of your customer things can change. A major factor here may be Timing, which will be covered in a later chapter.

My aircraft charter company multiplied in size mostly on the strength of just one customer—General Motors. When they had a fifteen percent cut back in production, we had an eighty-five percent cutback. Even their top management did not know how long this slowdown would last, and they warned me not to put all of my eggs in their basket. However, I decided to maintain my pilot staff and ground crews knowing that just two weeks of GM's business would overcome two months of losses from my over staffing. It was a gamble motivated out of my desire to keep the GM business, which I knew I could only do if I were ready when they needed me.

The slowdown lasted for months beyond anyone's expectations, and it soon had my little company on the ropes. At the last minute we went out and got more business which seemed to have saved us. But we were so weakened, when it was determined that we owed a vendor $20,000 when we had projected that they would owe us, that little $40,000 swing sunk the ship. There had been single *days* when we had made $40,000, but at that critical time, the way that it came threw us into insolvency.

With my 20/20 hindsight wisdom I now know that management decisions should always be founded upon circumstances as they **are** and not as you expect, or hope for them to be. This is not to say that projections and studies, or even hope, should not influence decisions, but they should rarely be the *foundation* for such decisions.

JUST THE FACTS PLEASE

Your Marketing division will almost always see things with more optimism than the ultimate reality justifies. You want them to be optimistic because that is the motivation that keeps them producing. Usually the optimism of a sales force is honest; they convey things the way they really see them, but they do tend to see through "rose colored glasses."

If their faith has been combined with patient endurance, they may actually impose their faith upon reality and make it happen as they see it. Therefore their optimism becomes reality. This combination of faith and patience is rare, but needed—it is built upon the resolve to overcome difficulties and turn failures into opportunities. However, true faith is an accurate appraisal of the way things are, combined with vision and hope for the way things can be. Combining the ability to face present realities as they are, with the faith to see the possibilities, is fundamental to building a successful Marketing team. Hype may get short term results, but will almost always result in ultimate decline or failure.

Good accountants will usually be overly conservative just as good salesmen will be overly optimistic. A good manager will listen to both of them, but not let either of them dictate policy. Both of these should have input into Marketing efforts. If you are a one man show, think about how much advertising could help you grow and then look at your checkbook before deciding how much to spend. Usually your best choice will be found somewhere between these two extremes of thought you just exercised.

THE BEST PROMOTIONS

Your success can depend upon how effectively you get the word out about your Product. There are many options available for doing this, but you must determine what will be the most effective and appropriate. Somehow I just would not feel comfortable with a brain surgeon who must have a billboard to advertise his services. There are Products whose best, and in some cases *only,* appropriate Marketing is through the recommendations of satisfied customers, reputation, and a track record of success. These will all be Products of the greatest importance and highest standards of integrity.

If this is true, then why not base the foundation of our Marketing upon recommendation, reputation and a track record. Of course, there may be many other aspects included in the Marketing of different Products, but should this not be our basic strategy? If we are unable to get recommendations, or our reputation is not something we can Market, that should reflect a basic need to change our Product, Administration or even the enterprise.

ENDORSEMENTS WITH CLASS

There is a reason why endorsements are one of the most effective advertising strategies. It is the same reason why the endorsements of well known media or sports personalities do not come cheap. The endorsement of a well known personality can be effective on television, but the endorsement of one satisfied customer to another potential customer will be a more solid foundation for continued success.

Effective Marketing only comes with good planning, just as effective Products do. You should develop a strategy for cultivating promotion by your satisfied customers. You can get statements from them that can be used in brochures and other advertisements. Ask them if you can use them as a reference for other prospects.

Even better than an endorsement may be a recommendation. A recommendation is more than just an endorsement, it is a "lead" which will almost certainly give you the attention of the potential new customer. This is something you will probably have to ask your satisfied customer to do for you but few will mind if they really are satisfied, or if you do give incentives for new business generated this way, such as a reward or discount. Just ask them if they know anyone else that can use your Product or service, and ask them if you can say that they recommended that you contact them. If you have a good enough relationship you might even ask them if they would mind contacting the prospect on your behalf. In short, **do not overlook what is potentially your most effective Marketing resource—your present customers.**

There are a couple of basic rules you should follow if you are going to use endorsements or recommendations:

1) Be sure that the one whose endorsement you are using has a good reputation. Even though someone may be a good and satisfied customer that does not mean that they are respected in their field. Some associations can *hurt* you.

2) Never use someone else's name as an endorsement or recommendation if you have not cleared it with that person, or you may well lose an established customer.

HONOR YOUR AMBASSADORS

Another basic principle for success in Marketing is that the effectiveness of your Marketing team will be directly related to the amount of esteem and reward given to them. Salesmen may be the most berated professionals, and are often the butt of jokes even by their own companies; yet they may well be the most important reason for success, or failure of that company.

Your salesman is your *ambassador*. Only the most foolish and backward governments will send out ambassadors who they do not esteem or respect. Just as an ambassador will speak for his government your salesman will speak for your company. He *is* your company to those he meets on your behalf. He *is* the impression that potential customers will have of *you*.

THE ESSENTIAL SKILL

Relating to other human beings may be the most difficult task we all have. From the time there were just two brothers in the world, Cain and Abel, they could not get along. The skill of meeting a new person, gaining their trust and selling them a Product, is not an easy task. The sales positions in your enterprise should be held in the highest esteem if you want ambassadors of the highest quality.

Esteem is usually measured by the attention given by the boss. If the boss is a true leader he will naturally give most of his time to those who are most important. Attention can be more effective in motivating your sales force than even raises or commissions. Good salesmen are usually paid well; they do not need money as much as they need respect. Give it to them and they will pay you back many times.

It is also more important for a salesman to believe in the Product than to just have a good personality, unless you are building your distribution on mere hype. Knowledge of the Product is essential if one is to really believe in it. The more knowledge a salesperson has of the Product, the more confident they will be in promoting it. Knowledge is a most important tool for the true Marketing professional. The investment you make in the education of your Marketing team will usually pay great dividends.

THE RIGHT START

Proper dress is also essential for Marketing professionals. The first impression your prospect will have of you will probably be of your clothes. If you are Marketing your Product to professionals, or successful businessmen, they will almost certainly judge you by your overall appearance. Conservative dress is almost always appropriate; you will seldom offend someone by being too conservative; you can easily offend someone by being too flashy or casual. Being over-dressed is easier to compensate for than being underdressed; it is easier to loosen your tie or take off your jacket to look casual than it is to put on a tie in front of your prospect. Casual clothes may be more appropriate for selling pleasure boats or sports equipment, but being neat and conservative is always appropriate.

A course in basic manners can pay high dividends for your Marketing team. Not only do good manners almost always give a positive impression, the basic knowledge of good manners also imparts social confidence—an essential for the successful Marketing Professional.

Learning to listen well is just as important as learning to speak well when it comes to professional salesmanship. Few things will turn off a busy executive or entrepreneur faster than a salesman who does not hear what they are trying to tell them. Learning to remember names or other personal details can be more than helpful—it is essential. It shows that you have listened and that you care. It also shows your prospect that if he has problems with your product, he has a personal contact who will help him receive the proper service.

IBM grew to be one of the greatest companies in the world. It had the right product at the right time, and dominated its industry in the fastest growing market of its time to such a degree that every other product was measured by how it compared to IBM's. However, IBM opened thc door for a catastrophic slide of historic proportions, mainly because they failed to listen to their own customers. When the computer industry made a major turn, IBM missed it. For several years now they have been trying to get back to where they missed the turn to get on the right road. Even if they do, their competitors are now pretty far down that road, and will be hard to catch.

CHARACTER TRAITS OF THE GOLDEN SALESMAN

It takes a unique person to do well in sales and promotions. There are certain general personality characteristics typical of those who are drawn to this profession. Some are strengths and some are weaknesses. Understanding these characteristics can help to accentuate the strengths, and overcome the weaknesses. Understanding these can also help those who must relate to them to do so more effectively. Below are a listing of each. Strengths are indicated with a (+), and weaknesses are indicated with a (–). Understand that these are generalizations and all of them may not apply to every individual.

(+) They Enjoy Life.
Marketing professionals usually have a good perspective on why they are doing this in the first place. Their

intrigue with events and general interest in life is contagious, and can help pull others out of the doldrums. They tend to be friendly, to genuinely enjoy, and be interested in other people. They will be quick to notice and help those in need. They can contribute greatly to morale. Even in difficult circumstances they will often crack a joke which helps to relieve the pressure, which often helps to get a proper perspective on the situation. Others like to be with them and they are the life of most parties. They can even make others enjoy being at work, which can have a significant impact on productivity.

(–) They Are Easily Distracted
They will tend to waste a lot of their time and other's by talking or playing games. Because they are so high on enjoying life, when the joy is gone often they will be too. They can be just as quick to commit themselves to other emotions than joy. They will fall in love faster, but also be quick to get a divorce. They can leave a trail of disappointed people, broken relationships, and bitter enemies. Because they run on positive emotions, they may run from problems and seldom resolve disputes that require confrontation.

Remedy
They need to work with, and have the influence of, those who are disciplined and deliberate in their leadership and lifestyle. If they can be kept focused, they will be your most productive people. Challenge their commitments by presenting potential problems and difficulties. Give them time to think about what they are committing to before you accept their commitment.

(+) Optimistic
They will quickly see potential where others only see

problems. They see opportunity and will initiate profitable ventures which others will not even notice.

(–) Tend To Be Emotional

They are often subject to emotional burnout, or even breakdowns. Because they are often overly optimistic they are often disappointed. Because they tend not to see problems, when one finally gets their attention it is usually a greater shock to them than it would be to others. Their "downs" can be just as extreme as their "ups." This can also make them prone to addictions. They are often subject to financial problems because they can buy on impulse and overcommit themselves when they are emotionally high, but avoid paying the bills because it is such an emotional low.

Remedy

The same as above. They need to be teamed with someone who is disciplined and guided by rationale rather than emotion.

(+) They Will Have High Energy

They will usually work hard and long. They will be quick to volunteer or tackle a hard task which will stimulate others to do the same.

(–) They Tend To Leave Jobs Unfinished

They are so quick to volunteer or start something that they often overload themselves with projects they cannot finish. They will be utterly sincere when they make their commitments, and fully intend to carry them out. However, because they tend to run on emotions, after the high emotional charge of starting something new has passed they can lose interest and easily be diverted. Because of this they may tend to change jobs frequently. They can be subject to procrastination because they want to do so many things they cannot decide between them. They are usually fast starters, but slow finishers.

Remedy
They need a rigid system of accountability, and they must learn to say "NO." They need strong leadership and management. Expect less than they promise so that you will not be disappointed. Make them accountable to clean up every mess they make—especially in human relations.

After reading the above one may be tempted to wonder if those of this temperament are worth the trouble. They are, and they may well become your most valuable people *if you understand them*, and learn to work with them to use their strengths and deal with their weaknesses. They can propel your enterprise to heights you would never otherwise attain, but they will not be able to keep you there.

The Bible is without equal in illuminating human character and disposition. The Apostle Peter is one of the great character sketches of those with the temperaments to be drawn to the Marketing profession. Peter was the first to proclaim the good news of the Christ, but he was also the first to desert when discouraging circumstances arose.

Peter did not desert because of cowardice; the very night before he denied Jesus he had charged an entire Roman cohort *by himself.* A Roman cohort was 800 men! These personality types are prone to discouragement, but not cowardice.

It was Peter who walked on the water, but he also sank once he got out there. They are often encouraged too quickly, and discouraged too quickly, but they are also restored quickly. Just a few weeks after his greatest failure Peter preached his greatest sermon. He had been given the keys to open the door because he would use them. Give them a job and these will not fail you in getting off to a good start. Peter could start the church, but a Paul was needed to establish it and give it endurance. This personality type can be a great leader, but a poor manager. Do not expect more of them than you should and your typical Marketing professionals will be some of your most valuable people.

DISTRIBUTION

The most effective Promotions can be completely undone by a poor Distribution system. The excitement of a new Product disappears quickly if it is too difficult to acquire. Modernization has afflicted the world with an addiction to convenience. A major portion of the success of any enterprise will now be determined by how convenient it is to acquire the Product. Your distribution system needs to be as well planned and executed as your Promotions.

I link Promotions and Distribution because of how directly they will impact each other. Who will your Product appeal to? If it will appeal to a wide spectrum of society you may want to do some promotional spots on a country music station and sell it through K-Mart or Walmart. If your Product is likely to only appeal to the very wealthy you may want to promote it on a classical music station and distribute it through a more ritzy department or specialty store. Your Promotion strategy should work in harmony with your Distribution strategy.

Because of its convenience, direct mail has become an increasingly popular method of distribution. When a consumer computes the value of his time, the cost of shipping is usually less than the cost of shopping. But stocking your Product in a store is one method of promoting it; every time someone walks by and sees it your Product has been promoted. If you are going to distribute through direct mail, you must devise other effective methods of Promotion to get your potential customer's attention.

The most effective Marketing will be a blend of Promotion and Distribution. If you look at them together you will have a greater tendency to keep them in balance. Do not ever forget that the best Promotions in the world will be undone by poor Distribution. In a sense, these two are a combination of Leadership (Promotions) and Management (Distribution). You need them both and you need them working together.

Chapter Thirteen

Resources

You can have the best Product, the best Administration, the best Marketing and perfect Timing, but the lack of adequate **Resources** can be the doom of your enterprise. Resources include Capital and any other materials required for your venture.

Capital is essential to every venture. You are not going anywhere without some of it; you are not going very far without enough of it. The lack of proper capitalization is the number one reason for business failure in America.

Also, some of the easiest ways to obtain capital for starting a business can also be the seeds for your ultimate destruction. Every business is in business to make money, but many who are in business do not really understand money. If you are the typical entrepreneur, this is your number one problem. Regardless of what your venture is, your Resources are probably your greatest concern. In this chapter we will offer a reasonable, workable plan for changing that. If you follow it, you can change this great problem into the least of your concerns, which should result in the redirection of your energies into areas that will bear more, and lasting, results.

THE LIFE IS IN THE BLOOD

Your capital resources are the life blood of your enterprise. If you are anemic in your supply of capital all of the other essentials will be weakened by it. If this flow is restricted you will be in constant danger of a heart attack in your venture. If you receive a "transfusion" from a bad source it can afflict or kill you.

You must watch over the condition of your capital supply just as you would your own blood and coronary system. You should not begin the enterprise until you have an adequate supply, and a workable plan to keep it flowing. Neither should your plan to keep it flowing depend on optimistic income projections. There are places to be optimistic in business, but this is not one of them.

HELPFUL PROFESSIONALS

Bankers can help you establish a plan for your enterprise, but you must understand that bankers seldom really understand business; if they did they would not be in banking, they would be in business. What bankers do understand is crucial to business, which is how to keep the "life blood" of capital flowing through your venture. However, you must help your bankers resist trying to help you too much, and try to run your business for you.

Accountants can be a great help in laying a solid financial plan for your venture, but understand that few accountants really understand business. Even so, what accountants do understand is also crucial to business. In essence, accountants can help you monitor how healthy the life blood of your venture is. Even so, you must help your accountants resist trying to run your business for you.

Likewise, few lawyers really understand business, but what they do understand can also be crucial to your venture.

However, you must also help them resist trying to run your business.

All of these professionals are like physicians who can give your business needed checkups, and who can help you stay on the path to remaining healthy, so you should listen to them—only do not let them run your life. Some of these professionals are shrewd businessmen and women, but they are rare. Far more common are those who think that they are shrewd businessmen because they have so much interaction with them, but who really do not understand the whole business picture.

If your professionals are typical, they will be conservative to the point of irritating the average entrepreneur. There is a proverb that says, "The blows of a friend are better than the kisses of an enemy." Most of your meetings with your banker or accountant will end up being a blow to your plans and your ego, but they are the blows of a genuine friend that may well save you from the fatal blows of defeat.

However, you probably would not even be the leader of your enterprise if you were as conservative as these professionals tend to be, and you will probably not be very successful if you are overly conservative. Seldom is a great advance made by any enterprize without stepping out into the deep waters of *risk*. You must not let your professional counselors keep you from going where you must go to advance. Even so, if you listen to them, they will at least help keep you aware of the traps and dangers that you may not know are out there. Even if you are going to sail in those waters, you do need to know about the dangers.

COMMON MISTAKES

It is not possible to do a comprehensive study of Capitalization in this one chapter, but we will try to highlight a few of the more common mistakes, or missed opportunities, that are made in relation to this Essential area of your venture.

Mistake #1 for many is the failure to study and understand General Accounting Principles (GAP). "Accounting" means just that—the ability to *account* for your resources. If you cannot account for them you will have hemorrhages. Just as continual bleeding will weaken any person, and ultimately kill them, the failure to use proper accounting principles will do the same for your enterprise.

Just as not using GAP can lead to loss, using them will lead to strengthening your entire organization. They will give you new insights into efficient management strategies and possibilities. In short, GAP can help your overall planning and organization. Using GAP keeps your hand on the pulse of your enterprise, alerting you to problems, and letting you move more quickly to take advantage of opportunity.

The remedy for this common problem is to study and understand GAP before your start your enterprise, and discipline yourself to continually increase your knowledge of them. Most entrepreneurs are concept oriented people—visionaries, who get bored with details and try to avoid dealing with them. It requires discipline to study and keep up with the accounting, but you desperately need that discipline, and the knowledge that you will derive from it.

Probably the second biggest mistake made by entrepreneurs is the dependence upon too much debt for Capitalization. If you have borrowed money to capitalize at fifteen percent interest, you must make an *extra* fifteen percent profit just to pay the interest. Debt is sometimes the only alternative, but it should be considered a last alternative whenever possible, unless the interest rates are extremely low.

The remedy is to idealistically make the ultimate goal of your enterprise to be debt free. When starting your enterprise consider other means of capitalization, such as a private stock offering, limited partnership, etc. They all have positives and negatives, but few of the negatives are as bad as debt.

If you must go into debt to start your venture, have a primary goal to be out of debt within a specific period of time. Otherwise you will become addicted to what amounts to a very bad, and costly drug habit.

To get out of debt as fast as you can is as simple as building your own reserves for emergencies, general needs and "venture capital." How can you do this? It will take intelligence, discipline, determination and courage. The speed with which you accomplish it is not as important as the consistency, so make your time goal realistic. The following is an example of a simple, brief, but workable plan for getting out of debt.

Step #1. Do not borrow any more money. Pay off existing debt. The temptation to just keep on borrowing should be considered the same as just getting one more fix. You may be able to rationalize just one more, but then you will keep on doing it. This addiction will ultimately destroy your venture.

You may think that this is just the way that almost everyone does business now, and it is true that just about all entrepreneurs now have this addiction. Now the whole business world is in slavery to the few who had the smarts to be the suppliers, not the addicts. If you are going into business, do not subject yourself to this slavery! If you are in slavery now, get out!

Step #2. Build your reserves. Put one percent of gross income into an Emergency Fund which is not to be touched except to avoid default. After the Emergency Fund has reserves enough to cover your entire budget for three to six months, add this one percent to the General Reserve Fund.

Put two percent of gross income into a General Reserve Fund which should not be used except for serious and defined needs. After this account has enough funds to cover all expenses for an additional six months to a year of operations, take this three percent (One percent from the Emergency account that is now funded) and begin building a Venture

Fund for taking advantage of opportunities without borrowing.

Almost any enterprise, charity, church, or family can operate on ninety-seven percent of its income without even missing the three percent used to build these reserves. If you cannot do this you are living too close to the precipice of financial catastrophe. These reserves can help prevent having to borrow money on short notice, which usually involves higher interest rates, and can put a deadly strain on the heart of your venture.

Step #3. Learn to live on less. Have a goal of each year putting an additional two percent into your reserves. In just five years you will have almost painlessly learned to make it on less than ninety percent of your income. If possible do it faster than this, but *consistency over time is the key to your financial health.*

Step #4. Learn to manage your assets properly. Use the time value of money to your advantage, not the bank's. Let's take a hypothetical look at what can be done with the reserve accounts of a small enterprise that has a consistent gross income of just $100,000 per year, and uses the conservative approach of putting away just three percent, or $3,000 per year. Figure 3 gives the value of that small deposit at different interest rates over time. If your gross income is $200,000 you can double these numbers. If it is $1,000,000 you can multiply them by 10.

These numbers may seem wildly exaggerated to one who does not understand the time value of money, or the effect that just a couple of percentage points can make on the ultimate return with compounding interest. Bankers know these figures very well, which is why they usually have the biggest buildings in town. Over 40 years just 2% difference in the compounded interest rate can mean about 100% difference in the total return. The difference between 14% and 16% in this example is $6,543,891 or just at 100%.

	10%	12%	14%	16%
10 years	$54,642	$62,211	$71,055	$81,405
	Total Investment — $30,000			
15 years	$111,252	$136,221	$167,892	$208,402
	Total Investment — $45,000			
20 years	$205,227	$272,193	$364,773	$493,509
	Total Investment — $60,000			
30 years	$620,232	$1,088,925	$1,578,915	$2,579,802
	Total Investment — $90,000			
40 years	$1,763,943	$3,373,062	$6,597,783	$13,141,674
	Total Investment — $120,000			

** Figures do not compute the effect of taxes or other costs.

Figure 3 – 3% Savings For Gross Annual Income of $100,000

THE SKILL OF INVESTING

Your ability to invest your resources properly will almost certainly have as much to do with your ultimate value, or net worth, as your ability to make money. Most of those who are good at making money are not very good at investing it.

If you have a "CD" (Certificate of Deposit), after looking at the scale above you are probably wondering where you can get 16% return on your money safely. There are a number of quality, safe investment vehicles (such as some mutual funds) that average that much or better. The small amount of time that it takes to understand and begin to use such investment vehicles can ultimately pay much greater dividends on your time than you are making while managing your enterprise.

There are professional brokers and money managers who can help you, but there is no substitute for your own study and understanding of investment and money management. It is probable that if you are good at making money you do not have much time to manage your money, and will need the services of a broker. If you use a broker, you will still need to be able to judge between the good ones and bad ones, and there are plenty of bad ones. The time spent understanding asset management will probably pay at least as high a dividend to your ultimate net worth as the time spent actually making the money—and there is a probability that it will mean a whole lot more to your overall financial condition.

It is easy to see how discipline and consistency over a period of time can enable even a small enterprise to begin financing itself. This should be your ultimate goal. The closer you get to this, the healthier your financial position will be. Instead of paying the lenders most of your profits, they can be compounding in your own account, multiplying the ultimate fruit of your labors.

Where would the average business, church, ministry or government be if they had instituted a simple, conservative plan of putting away reserves in order to ultimately finance their own growth? The fact is that the average church in America, which has existed for more than forty years, would never have to go to the bank again to finance its growth, and could probably finance the starting of new churches and ministries. Most governments, which have been in existence even longer, would almost never have to even consider borrowing, or issuing bonds, and would be in a position to give much better incentives to new industries and businesses who locate in their region.

THE TIME VALUE OF MONEY

If a young couple that marries at age 25 just funds their IRA's, putting away $4,000 per year ($2,000 each), they will have over $2,000,000 at their retirement (age 65), if they get a 10% annual return on their investment. If they are a little more aggressive and get 14% they will have almost $9,000,000. If they get 16% they will have over $17,000,000, which is $15,000,000 more than they would have at a 10% return.

It should be the goal of every family to live on less than 75% of its net income. If your family makes $40,000 a year, live as if you make $30,000. Take a couple of raises and promotions without raising your standard of living for just a few years. If you have the resolve and discipline to do this, soon you will be able to leap into a much higher standard of living without staying on the thin edge of financial disaster.

The average family pays interest on loans that equals many times what they end up with in their nest eggs for retirement. With just a little planning, discipline, and restraint for a few years that can be reversed—you can have many times the amount in your savings that you have paid in interest to banks or other lenders. Again, debt must be thought of as a deadly addiction.

WISDOM WITH DEBT

Now it is true that few businesses could ever begin without some debt. If you want to play in the enterprise game, you will almost certainly have to go into debt. However, it is important to view all debt as bad, and use it only when it is absolutely necessary, understanding the biblical proverb, "The borrower is the lender's slave." Our goal should always be to get out of slavery just as fast as we can, which means to pay off our debt, and stay out of debt.

There is some debt that it may be wise to take, such as a mortgage in an area where real estate values can be expected to appreciate. Sometimes mortgage payments are close to what you would have to pay to rent comparable property, so why not be buying it? The tax advantage of writing off the interest can also be a factor in this. However, this tax advantage should not be absolutely counted on, but be thought of as a bonus. All tax advantages can be subject to change.

Even with the tax advantages, if you buy into a real estate market that has peaked and values will be depreciating, a home mortgage can be a poor long term investment. Of course, there are other factors in making a real estate investment, such as needing the property, or just liking it enough to be willing to lose some money on it. Real estate can, during certain types of economic conditions, be a good hedge against inflation. However, it is always wise to pay off your debt ASAP.

The riskiest form of debt is speculation debt. If you have an investment vehicle that you consistently get a 20% return on, it may be in your interest to borrow some money that you only pay 8% on to put into this vehicle, as you will be making 12% on the borrowed money. Of course, the amount of debt assumed for this purpose should be balanced with the highest standard of safety and liquidity of the investment vehicle. It should also be your goal to pay off the borrowed money ASAP.

CONTRARY INVESTING

The basic, successful, investment strategy is to buy low and sell high. For the long term investor this often means doing the opposite of what the crowd is doing; you have to buy what is not in favor at the time, and sell when it comes into favor and everyone else is buying. If you are buying a commodity that is cyclical, you buy when it is down, and sell when it is up.

Most newspapers list the 52 week *high* and *low* prices for stocks. Some of the most successful investors simply look for *quality* stocks that are at or near their 52 week low price, buy them, and then wait until they reach their 52 week high price to sell them. Some stocks will fluctuate as much as 50% or more of their value between these highs and lows, and some will hit each several times a year. If you buy low and sell high with just a 25% spread four times in a year, you will have doubled your investment. If it just happens once you will have made 25%, which is not bad by most standards.

Of course, any investing does involve risk, and usually the greater the potential return, the greater the risk. It is not wise to make any such investments with money that you cannot afford to lose. Those without patience, and the willingness to suffer "paper losses" for awhile should not play this game either. You may buy a stock right at its 52 week low price, but it could be going lower than that. It is wise to study every company that you are going to invest in to look for trends that might make its prices head even lower than they have been within the last year. That is where the next investment strategy can be helpful.

DOLLAR COST AVERAGING

The investment strategy called "Dollar Cost Averaging" can be most effective if you are investing for the long term. This strategy requires investing the same amount of money in a targeted investment vehicle at regular time intervals. Lets take an exaggerated example of this in order to illustrate the effect of this simple, but relatively safe and effective strategy.

Let's pretend to invest $100 per month in a company whose stock is trading at $10 per share when we begin, but drops $1 a share per month until it has lost 90% of its value. It then stays flat for 6 months before rising just $1 a share per month until it regains just half of its original value. As Figure 4 shows, what appears to be a bad loser actually results in a 142% return on your investment if you are faithful to the Dollar Cost Averaging Strategy.

This is an exaggerated example meant to dramatize the effect of Dollar Cost Averaging. There are not many investment vehicles that will be this consistent in their downward or upward performance. One must also consider the stress that he may endure the entire time that his investment is down, because there is no guarantee that it will ever come back up.

Month	Cost of Stock	Shares Bought	Shares Owned	Total Invest.	Invest. Value	Gain <Loss>	
1	$10	10	10	$100	$100	–0–	
2	$9	11	21	$200	$190	<$10>	-5%
3	$8	13	34	$300	$272	<$28>	-9%
4	$7	14	48	$400	$336	<$64>	-16%
5	$6	17	65	$500	$390	<110>	-22%
6	$5	20	85	$600	$425	<175>	-29%
7	$4	25	110	$700	$440	<260>	-37%
8	$3	33	143	$800	$429	<371>	-46%
9	$2	50	193	$900	$386	<514>	-57%
10	$1	100	293	$1000	$293	<707>	-70%
11	$1	100	393	$1100	$393	<707>	-64%
12	$1	100	493	$1200	$493	<707>	-59%
13	$1	100	593	$1300	$593	<707>	-54%
14	$1	100	693	$1400	$693	<707>	-51%
15	$1	100	793	$1500	$793	<707>	-47%
16	$2	50	843	$1600	$1686	$86	5%
17	$3	33	876	$1700	$2628	$928	54%
18	$4	25	901	$1800	$3604	$1804	100%
19	$5	20	921	$1900	$4605	$2705	142%

** Fractions and cents are rounded.

Figure 4 – The Effects of Dollar Cost Averaging

However, for long term investments using this strategy *you want the price to fall while you are buying,* allowing you to purchase more shares or units for your money. This will result in paper losses for this time, but you really do not want the price to start rising until you intend to sell. The key to this strategy is consistency and patience. I used months in this example, but you can change that to days, weeks, or years, as long as it is consistent, and the amount of the regular investment is consistent.

With this example comes the temptation to just wait for the investment vehicle to bottom out before buying shares. This is almost impossible for even the most astute investor to do. The bottom could be reached at any point along the descent, and the top reached at any point in the ascent. Dollar Cost Averaging helps you to use the *averages* to benefit from either a descending or an ascending investment.

Obviously, to benefit from a descending investment you must have the resolve, and the capital, to stick with it until it has made a positive turn. It takes a great deal of courage to do this, and it definitely is not for everyone. It is also recommended that you only use "risk capital" with such a strategy.

I can testify to the fact that I have personally used this investment strategy with my retirement account for the last few years. I have used it with the stocks of over a dozen companies, and I have not yet lost on a single company that I have invested in. I have done as well as doubling my return on investment in a company in just two months. However, I do not intend to draw from my retirement account for over twenty more years, so I will not be overly concerned if we should enter a "bear" (downward) market that lasts ten years or more—in fact it would suit me just fine because I would be able to buy more shares for my investment.

A WARNING

There are also some signs that our entire market economy could be in serious jeopardy of total collapse because of the national debt. I am watching for signs that should give at least some warning that this is imminent, in which case I would be quick to sell my investments. Even so, there is no guarantee that these signs will give the necessary warning before a catastrophic collapse. Even though the U.S. may be the strongest and healthiest economy in the world (which is now debatable), the entire world's economy is on very shaky ground, and some financial earthquakes are likely.

However, in some ways wealth is like energy: it is never destroyed, it just changes forms. In the case of wealth, whenever there is a catastrophic collapse, wealth is not destroyed, it just changes hands, and the hands that it changes to are the ones who are prepared for it. Those who will be in the position to take advantage of the coming, worldwide, economic collapse will be those who are out of debt with a strong asset base. The timing of this collapse is debatable, but it is inevitable without drastic changes in government policies, which no government has yet been willing to make.

THE OTHER SIDE OF DEBT

On the other side of reducing your own debt for a more healthy capital position, is reducing the debt that is owed to you—your Accounts Receivable. Many businesses that were successful in developing a quality Product, and effectively getting it to the market failed because they extended credit too freely and could not collect their receivables. Those who owe you are using your money as working capital. You may well be having to pay the bank interest on the same amount of operating capital on which those who owe you are using to collect interest. If you are paying the bank 12% interest on a working capital loan, and could be earning 12% on that money properly invested that is a 24% swing in your capital flow (Remember how much just a few interest points can mean to you over time.).

The best credit policy is written on our money, "In God we trust"—*for all others cash!* Of course this policy is not always feasible. Often your best customers will insist on credit. There are many factors to be considered but you should have as a goal to stay as close to zero in your receivables as possible. This will require planning and consistency.

POSITIVE COLLECTING

There are positive and negative incentives that you can use as effective coercion to bring in your receivables and keep them low. The positive incentives will make your customers happy; the negative ones will often make them mad, but they can both work. Since you do not want to make your good customers angry, you probably want to use the positive incentives until you have to use the negative ones.

A positive incentive could be a discount for prepayment with another lesser discount for quick payment. These have proven very effective. An effective way to keep this option in the mind of your customers is to print two totals on the invoice—the lower one if paid by a certain date, and the other one if paid after that date.

You can also give respect as an incentive. Send your best payers a "Gold Credit" recognition letter for their prompt payments. Send those who are the next level down in their performance a "Silver Credit" letter, thanking them for their good standing, while tactfully letting them know that there is a "Gold" rating. Let all of your customers know that you have such a rating system. This may sound too easy, but it does work. Good business people are success oriented, competitive, and want to achieve the highest rating possible. If there is no reward, or penalty, they are also smart enough to use your money for as long as they can.

NEGATIVE COLLECTING

There is a point at which you must determine that your positive incentives are not working with someone. Then you may need to become increasingly negative in your approach to recover what is owed to you. Most businesses have an automatic one and a half percent charge added to the invoice after thirty days and for each additional thirty days the payment is late. Notations on the invoice such as "OVERDUE" can help. A phone call will often get a response.

After these methods have been used without success there are collection agencies, lawyers, credit bureaus, etc. However, the more extreme the measures you have to use to collect your receivables, the more likely you are to lose the customer. You have to decide at which point they are not a desirable customer anyway. The one who is buying the most from you is hurting you more than anyone if he is not paying you.

The credit that you are going to extend through your enterprise should be well planned, systematic and consistent. If you yield in charging the penalties they will not be effective, *and* you will also lose the respect of your customers. If the credit you are willing to extend is the main selling point to a prospective customer you probably do not need his business.

It is almost always best to let quality and value, not credit, be your reasons for getting business, unless you are in the credit business. There are a number of major corporations who simply require that they be given longer to pay if you want their business, and their business may well be worth it. You may need the flexibility to make special deals but overall, if you do not effectively manage your receivables, they will probably end up affecting your enterprise in many ways, none of which are good.

SUMMARY

There are many other successful, easy to understand investment strategies. If you are going to build reserves you do need to have a plan for managing them properly. If you are just putting them in the bank you could well be losing the real value of your money just to inflation. Regardless of how good you are at producing growth for your venture, or making money, if you do not manage your assets properly you can end up with just a fraction of what you could have had. This is not meant to be a comprehensive study of asset management, but simply an encouragement for you to study it more thoroughly. The few hours you spend educating yourself about asset management will pay possibly greater dividends than anything else in the field of business and management that you spend your time on.

In almost any enterprise there will be timely opportunities that come your way that cannot wait for you to become strong enough financially to self-finance. In these cases debt may be a viable option for you. Even so, it may not be the only option and seldom should be considered your first option.

Most successful enterprises have been built more on shared ownership in the form of stock offerings, partnerships, etc., than on debt. Like debt, these forms of capitalization have positives and negatives. Most entrepreneurs are not wimps, they are independent thinkers, and are prone to action while others are still debating. Because of this they do not want to share control of their business, or venture and often just do not even want to answer to others. However, are you giving up even more long term control by going into debt?

There are ways to raise capital by selling a portion of your venture without losing control. As long as you maintain over 50% ownership you can maintain 100% of control unless you subjugate yourself under the terms of the offering. There are other ways, but using non-voting preferred or other classes of stock, that you can raise all of the capital that you need while not really losing any of the control, except for the greater scrutiny that you may be given by the Securities and Exchange Commission, and their scrutiny is often very helpful in keeping your venture within its proper limits.

As far as answering to others, most leadership types do not like to do this, but they do *need* to do it. There are people out there whose insight, knowledge and wisdom can help you. The most successful leaders are those who know how to listen. Learning to answer to others, and listen to their input, which anyone who has invested in your venture deserves to have, may prove invaluable to you. Just having to give an account for your actions can help you to sharpen and understand your reasons for the action, which may help you to see other possibilities, and pitfalls that you may not have seen otherwise.

If you decide that sharing ownership in your venture is the best way for you to raise capital there are still a number of ways that you can do this. You should know your options before making a decision. An attorney and CPA can often give you advice worth many times what you have to pay them (and that is usually quite a bit).

It could be that a partnership will be better for you than incorporating, or a private offering may be better than a public one. Who do you want to be part owners with you? One of your best options could be a plan that would encourage your customers to invest in your venture. This can be a great way to lock in their business. Of course, this can also be a two-edged sword; do you want those to have a voice in your management whose real interest is in keeping your prices low, etc.? To what degree will they have inside information? These are all factors that must be considered.

Managing your capital can mean just as much to the success of your enterprise as any other factor. If you do not control your Capitalization it will end up controlling you.

Chapter Fourteen

Timing

Timing is the last of the Five Essentials that we will cover, but by no means the least important. Proper Timing will almost certainly determine the quality of your Product, the efficiency of your Administration, the effectiveness of your Marketing, and the strength of your Capitalization. In essence, Timing will be one of the biggest factors in determining your success or failure.

Proper Timing is the result of one's ability to balance patience with decisiveness. Patience and decisiveness are often conflicting characteristics, but both require the one essential quality found in all true leaders—courage. Without courage proper Timing will be elusive. At times it will take just as much courage to wait for the proper Timing as it would to push ahead. At times it will take courage to push ahead to seize the moment, when the rest of the organization seems unprepared and is pressuring you to wait longer.

Courage is not the absence of fear; it is the ability to control fear. There are fears that are healthy. It is healthy to fear bullets when you are in a battle. The heroes who take decisive action in battles, or other crises, usually feel just as much fear as everyone else; they simply overrule it in order to take action. A certain amount of fear may help you to better understand your situation. The right kind of fear can be useful, but the decisive leader controls his fears; he does not let the fears control him. When fear begins to control you, it will begin to distort your evaluation of the situation, often resulting in improper action and bad Timing.

A MINNOW TURNS INTO A SHARK

T. Boone Pickens is a modern example of how leadership can balance patience and decisiveness. He became a genius for using Timing to his advantage. Pickens, the C.E.O. of tiny Mesa Petroleum, shocked the corporate world by announcing that he was going to take over giant Cities Service Corporation. Executives laughed over their cocktails as the proverbial minnow was chasing the whale. But after a few weeks they changed their tune and started calling the "minnow" a "shark!"

Cities Service tried to preempt Pickens by filing to take over Mesa but Pickens held his course. The minnow was not able to eat the whole whale but it got more than anyone thought that it could. The "minnow" turned "shark" then turned on the even bigger whales of Phillips and Gulf. No one was laughing now. The audacity and courage of Pickens and a handful of couch cowboys forced the world's oil industry to restructure. This restructuring was not all positive, but it was probably essential if the industry was to survive in the fast changing world of oil politics.

To the unsophisticated, this corporate takeover game began to look like a simple strategy to buy a small percentage of stock in a company, announce a takeover which drives up the stock, then sell the stock at a big profit, which is the way many takeovers ended. However, it is not quite that simple. Pickens had "bet the house" that he could eat the whale. He could have lost Mesa, and though he came out with hundreds of millions in winnings, he could easily have lost just as much.

Pickens' victories were something akin to Col. Travis of the Alamo persuading Santa Ana to surrender, and not only give up Texas but a good part of Mexico too! That did not happen without a brilliant plan—and an almost superhuman resolve under pressure to stick to that plan until his "Santa Ana" started believing he was surrounded. Pickens' victories against the other oil giants could be compared to the little band at the Alamo then persuading the rulers of Spain and Italy to pay them millions or they would do the same thing to them that they had done to Santa Ana.

Boone Pickens versus the oil industry really was a modern day David and his little sling shot attacking the giant Goliath. Not only did Goliath have his armor on, he had an awesome spear, sword and shield. David would get one good shot and he had better not hit him in the knee! The oil industry's massive wealth, army of lawyers, lobbyists, influence with judges, lawmakers and the press, stood against Pickens who seemed to have nothing more in his hand than a seemingly ridiculous little plan. When it appeared that the oil industry had never been stronger, Pickens saw a weak spot and with perfect Timing and accuracy he had the courage to throw the stone. They were never expecting such a shot!

Pickens looks brilliant now but had he been just a little bit off he would have looked equally stupid. If you are going to go for the big one you had better be good, and your Timing had better be perfect. Being able to see the weak spot often takes brilliance; being able to take advantage of it will require courage, skill and Timing.

THE COURAGE OF PATIENCE

At Waterloo, Napoleon pressed Wellington to his limits all day long. A dozen times it looked like all was lost for the allies but not once did the Duke panic and use his one "ace in the hole." Then, when the famous Old Guard marched to the center of the field to seal the victory for the French, with perfect Timing Col. Colborne's regiment emerged from the cornfield to turn what looked like certain defeat into one of the most decisive victories in history.

Wellington's patience in releasing Colborne's regiment required an extraordinary courage to resist pressure in crisis after crisis until the Timing was perfect. Over a dozen times that day his army was on the verge of collapse, when he must have been under the most extraordinary pressure to bring out these reinforcements, but he resisted. He was determined not to use them just to save himself from defeat, but to consummate the victory. As he so perfectly demonstrated in this most famous of all battles, Courage and Patience are brothers.

Until you have learned patience, your Timing in life will seldom be good. True patience is not the lack of resolve; it is the understanding and respect for Timing. This one Essential will separate many winners from the losers.

When you go down a street and see a footing being dug you know that a house or small building is soon to go up. But when you turn down a street and see the whole block fenced off, with a deep pit, and at the bottom of that pit men still driving pilings trying to find the bedrock, you know that a building of significance is going up there! For truly great and lasting results, we must build our enterprise or venture the same way. The more patience we have in laying a proper foundation, the more we will be able to build upon it. Patience, coupled with respect for Timing, will probably determine the degree of your success or failure. As the noted psychologist Carl Jung once said, "Hurry is not of the devil; it *is* the devil!" The devil is the enemy in Scripture, and *hurry* may well be the greatest enemy your enterprise will ever have.

THE COURAGE OF DECISIVENESS

Patience is fundamental to proper Timing, but decisiveness is no less necessary. Success is often achieved like a surfer catching a wave. In order for him to catch the wave he must first discern where the wave is going to break and position himself there. Then, when the right wave comes along, *he cannot hesitate*—if he does the wave will pass him by. To take advantage of opportunity, one must first discern where that opportunity is going to come and then position himself properly. Then, when that opportunity does come he must be ready to act—few will wait for long. If you have come so far as to be in the right place, at the right time, do not let hesitation kill your chance. Go for it!

SUMMARY

If it seems that this book has come to a conclusion that does not seem to be conclusive; please understand that this was the intention. This is meant to be but a cursory study of these basic principles of Leadership, Management and Five Essentials for success. There is a great deal more depth to the understanding of each of them than is presented in this brief study. I believe that the information provided here can be practical and useful, but my primary intention for presenting this book is to stimulate thought and further study. True leadership and quality management are a lifestyle, not just a course to be understood. This lifestyle requires the continual sharpening of one's skills and knowledge. When that ceases, your leadership, your management, and your life, will almost certainly be in retreat.

I do not have the academic credentials to be considered an expert on any of the subjects presented here. I merely have experience, both good and bad, which I have tried to convey in an interesting format to those who are seeking meaningful success. If this book has stimulated a desire for a deeper understanding of the subject matter, then it has accomplished its purpose.

Ask for your...

FREE

MorningStar
Resource Catalog

For a complete list of MorningStar Products
including books, teaching cassettes, music
cassettes and CDs, books on tape, journal
issues and much more, just write to:

**MorningStar Publications
16000 Lancaster Highway
Charlotte, NC 28277-2061**

... or call or fax us at:

**(800) 542-0278
(704) 542-0278
(704) 542-0280 (fax)**

MorningStar
PUBLICATIONS
16000 Lancaster Highway • Charlotte, NC 28277-2061